Praise for *The B*

"For years, Sheri Salata used her magical powers, work ethic, and generous spirit to make other people's lives better. Finally she had to learn how to turn that magic inward. *The Beautiful No* is a road map for transformation—an honest, funny, and soulful look at what it really means to take stewardship over your own existence."

> —Elizabeth Gilbert, *New York Times* bestselling author
> of *Eat, Pray, Love*

"Sheri Salata's journey to a life of extraordinary success ultimately triggered a transformation to wholeness and healing. Read this book, *The Beautiful No*, and be inspired to embark on your own journey of emotional and spiritual fulfillment."

> —Deepak Chopra, *New York Times* bestselling author
> of *The Seven Spiritual Laws of Success*, *You Are the Universe*,
> and *The Healing Self*

"In this bracingly honest, tenderhearted, profoundly human book, Sheri Salata peels back the layers of a life that, on the surface, looks like pure success, and tells the truth of what it is to struggle, to fear, to grieve, to desire—in other words, to live. *The Beautiful No* will make you laugh. It will make you cry. It will make you feel. It will make you want to be Sheri Salata's friend."

> —Dani Shapiro, *New York Times* bestselling author of
> *Inheritance: A Memoir of Genealogy, Paternity, and Love*

"I've always loved deeply personal stories that lead the reader to discover a new way of considering what they believe to be true about themselves. *The Beautiful No* delivers courage, honesty, and contagious reflection."

—Nate Berkus, celebrated designer and star of
Nate & Jeremiah by Design

"Sheri Salata has created a permission slip for us all. This book inspires me to love harder, live bolder, and just frickin' go for it. It will do the same for you, too."

—Kris Carr, *New York Times* bestselling author,
cancer thriver, and wellness activist

"Sheri takes us through her courageous journey from her brilliant career to stepping forward to find and live her most brilliant life. In every page of *The Beautiful No* rings a big YES of how worth it it is to go through whatever it takes to get to know the being we truly are."

—Agapi Stassinopoulos, author of *Wake Up to the Joy of You*

"This is a beautifully written page-turner that had me hooked. I was rooting for Sheri on every page and when I reached the end, I felt like I just had the best meeting with a new best friend."

—Arielle Ford, bestselling author of *Wabi Sabi Love*

"A must-read for anyone who is ready to take the leap to joy, freedom, forgiveness, and authenticity."

—Colette Baron-Reid, bestselling author of *The Map: Finding the Magic and Meaning in the Story of Your Life*

"There are few experiences in life where you leave feeling more connected, more aware of yourself than when you begin. Sheri's ability to tell her story in a way that feels universal and vibrationally relevant is nothing short of magical."

—Jeremiah Brent, celebrated designer and star of
Nate & Jeremiah by Design

"For thirty years, Sheri and I have been telling each other stories. This beautiful book of hers feels like every great conversation we've ever had—complete with laughs, tears, surprises, and moments of revelation. Her voice is one of a kind and her stories never fail to inspire. Pull up a chair, as I have done many times, and dive in."

—Nancy Hala, cofounder of The Pillar Life and
cohost of *The Sheri + Nancy Show*

"Sheri Salata tells a captivating story of the inner transformation it sometimes takes to shed your mind shadows so you can see your own brilliant light. Reading *The Beautiful No,* I realized that vulnerability is a superpower. And that Sheri is my hero."

—Gordana Biernat, bestselling author of *#KnowTheTruth*

The Beautiful No

The Beautiful No

And Other Tales of Trial,

Transcendence, and

Transformation

SHERI SALATA

HARPER WAVE

An Imprint of HarperCollins*Publishers*

FIRST HARPER WAVE PAPERBACK EDITION PUBLISHED 2021.

Designed by Leah Carlson-Stanisic

Illustration by SoulQuess/Shutterstock, Inc.

Library of Congress Cataloging-in-Publication Data has been applied for.

ISBN 978-0-06-274320-6

21 22 23 24 25   LSC   10 9 8 7 6 5 4 3 2 1

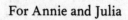

For Annie and Julia

Based on many, many true stories.

Contents

Foreword

M y first reading of *The Beautiful No: And Other Tales of Trial, Transcendence, and Transformation* was while on a plane to France, where I was heading to lead a retreat. My second reading was during a global pandemic—in my underwear on the living room floor of my one-bedroom apartment.

Through the lens of lockdown I returned to this book (which has become a bible for me) through a filter of appreciation. As Sheri Salata beautifully describes, "Appreciation brings presence, softens mourning, and offers a rising up."

I had found myself in a steaming pile of no and couldn't find the beauty in any of it until I reread her book.

My personal pile of no included, but was not limited to, losing all my income, not being able to see my mother and stepfather (for god knows how long) because they were immunocompromised, having to cancel a workshop Elizabeth Gilbert and I were hosting for women who worked for nonprofits, canceling the rest of my retreats, losing all my public speaking gigs, losing all the money I had paid for my son's overpriced preschool, and on and on.

I could not get out of bed. I was severely depressed and felt paralyzed by all the nos around me and in the world.

And wouldn't you know it, *The Beautiful No* was right there in a stack of books by my bedside under a children's book, *Dragons Love Tacos*. Don't get me wrong, I love *Dragons Love Tacos*, but it wasn't what I needed. I mean, everyone needs a taco, but what I needed to get me out of this funk was the voice of Sheri Salata.

Sheri and I shared a publication date for our books, and she'd become my book sister, my confidante, my talisman. I carried *The Beautiful No* in my suitcase to my retreats and workshops (next to a picture of my father because I believe fiercely in the power of our people), but I hadn't sat down to reread the whole book cover to cover without interruption. So I picked it up again.

Or let me rephrase: it picked me.

It picked me up.

I think life is a process of remembering—a constant remembering of who we really are—and as I reread Sheri's book, I began to remember. I got still. I had been running around and traveling and working for so long that I needed this stillness in order to take a good, hard look at myself. Thankfully, I had *The Beautiful No* as my companion or I am not sure I would have done it. In these pages, Sheri takes a good, hard look at herself and takes the reader along with her. Without shame.

Stuck in my one-bedroom apartment with nowhere to go but inward, I was scared. But I had this road map in my hands. Sheri Salata had walked this road, and she left a treasure map for us.

Spoiler alert: the treasure is ourselves.

I didn't realize I needed a reckoning until I reopened the book. I understood my own beautiful no was a pause of life as I knew it (albeit due to a deadly pandemic), and it was allowing me, or rather *forcing* me, to reckon with my own life.

However, I couldn't do it alone. I didn't *want* to. So I grabbed a highlighter and began my journey into *The Beautiful No* once again.

I call the voice in our head that tells us we aren't good enough "the Inner Asshole." *The Beautiful No* offers compassion, and what you will find, I am most certain, is that while reading it, your Inner Asshole will quiet itself. I noticed after the second reading that my own particular Inner Asshole stayed quiet for longer periods of time. I won't lie and say it's fully gone (just as Sheri doesn't lie in this book), but it has receded.

As promised, the softening came with the appreciation—as did the presence, and the rising up. I did eventually get out of bed.

Sometimes we need our friends to help get us out of bed.

I want to let you in on a secret. This book will be your friend. (Tacos may be your friend, too. You can have more than one friend, people.)

At some point, we all have to reckon with what we have made of our lives, and I can think of no better friend I would want on this trek. It's not always easy seeing the beauty in life, or in the no, so I thank the gods of books and coffee that this book is in the world to make it easier.

—Jen Pastiloff, author of the national

bestseller *On Being Human*

Tell Me Your Story
and I'll Tell You Mine

Jack Benny Junior High,
We proudly sing your name,
our teams will never yield
as they go down the field
they will lead us on to fame.

—"Jack Benny 39ers Fight Song," 1971

S o, this is my story.

It's about how a regular middle-class girl from Waukegan, Illinois, grows up to run one of the most beloved brands
on the planet and one of the most successful television shows
in history and then, after all that—after all that dreamy on-the-
job-ness—finally figures out how to live the life of her dreams.

Like any good story, it begins with a quest.

I wonder, all these years later, if my quest wasn't actually
launched in grade school. After my navy dad retired from

active duty, we settled in my parents' hometown: Waukegan, Illinois. This bustling mini-metropolis was an hour north of Chicago and claimed as its favorite son the legendary comedian of yore Jack Benny, who was quite famous for always saying he was thirty-nine years old. Hilarious stuff for its time. I was a proud "Jack Benny 39er," enrolled at the junior high institution that still bears his name. We Waukeganites really milked the Jack Benny connection, that is until another hometown hero, Jerry Orbach, hit the big time in the mega-hit TV series *Law & Order*.

It was in eighth grade that I had my first real brush with show biz. After years of waiting on "the list," my auntie Barb scored impossible-to-get tickets to *Bozo's Circus*, which taped in downtown Chicago at WGN Studios. I was entranced by the big studio cameras and even though I was the oldest "child" in the audience and twice as tall as the itty-bitties, I loved the energy of the live taping as the crew scurried around the set. There was a make-or-break tension that felt like life. I wasn't selected for the Grand Prize game but snagged the second most coveted spot on the show, introducing the cartoon. Mr. Ned, in his top hat and red tails, cozied on up to me in the bleachers as I proudly faced the camera and declared, "Folks, here's Huckleberry."

I was a born producer. In my earliest memories I am leading groups of my little pals in live productions of *Barbie, High*

School Musical (decades before the blockbuster movie), and *The Life and Times of Uncle and Aunt Sam* (it always bugged me that she was not represented) all involving acres of crunchy crepe paper, Elmer's glue, and the big box of Crayolas. As the oldest grandchild on both sides of my family, I was pretty much in charge while the adults were sipping their manhattans, martinis, and scotches. My brother and first cousins on both sides were my beloved cast for all of our family skits and musical spectaculars. Though they sometimes balked at my relentless rehearsal schedules, they always loved the standing ovations that came after. Everyone does.

Producing is multifaceted. First you have to be a bit of a visionary and love that "dreaming things up" process, and then it doesn't hurt if you like to herd kittens, as they say, because you are in charge of the whole shebang. But it is absolutely essential that you have real storytelling chops. I polished all of those skills in my spare time for most of my life and one magical day they led me to the greatest show on earth—*The Oprah Winfrey Show.*

The producers were arguably the most prolific storytellers in TV. And every kind of story under the sun got told in the hallowed halls of Harpo Studios. Spiritual stories, lesson stories, literary stories, famous-people stories, historic stories, giveaway stories, makeover stories, and the kind of deeply personal stories that could make you laugh out loud, shout "aha!," or bring you to "the ugly cry," as Oprah coined. People's stories mattered, and that is no doubt why untold millions tuned in around the world from every walk of life for twenty-five years.

As a writer and a producer, I have honored the impactful nature of stories for a long time, but it's only now in the middle of my life, that I understand their awesome quantum power. I can see clearly now that stories are the actual building blocks of our lives. They are the ingredients of our intentions, our deepest desires, our requests to the Universe, our hopes, our most fervent prayers. And the most crucial stories are the ones we author for an audience of one, ourselves. That's right, what we say *to* ourselves *about* ourselves—about every area of our lives—is life and death. The difference between the joy ride and the hard road.

It almost seems too simple, which is why I think we miss that nugget over and over again. I had a front-row seat to some of the most enlightened people on the planet (Deepak Chopra, Dr. Maya Angelou, Marianne Williamson, Iyanla Vanzant, Bishop Jakes, Eckhart Tolle, Cheryl Richardson, Gary Zukav, Wayne Dyer, Jack Canfield, Debbie Ford, Louise Hay, Geneen Roth, Dr. Phil, Dr. Oz, and the list goes on) sharing bushel baskets of wise pearls. And while I ate up every teaching, every word with a spoon, it's only now that I understand that the stories I tell myself matter more than anything. Believe me, it requires constant rewiring because those neural pathways of unconsciousness, at this stage of my life, have some well-worn grooves. I am as quick to put myself down, reach for guilt or shame like a Triscuit with French onion dip, as I ever was—but what I focus on now is catching the first few words of that deflating, cynical story before it becomes a paragraph. When I hear that dream-killing voice, I literally say out loud, "Not helpful . . . not helpful" (a life-changing tip from spiritual teacher Esther Hicks), as I snap myself back into the now.

Somehow we think of it as being vain or being too self-absorbed to tend to ourselves and our stories properly. To give ourselves the benefit of the doubt, the pat on the back, the word or two that raises our spirits and reminds us of how extraordinary and divine and beautiful we really are. I'm going to guess that you are like I was for so many years: you talk to your pets or to a stranger's baby in a grocery store with so much more love than you have ever spoken to yourself.

There are a lot of supportive choices you can make—heart-opening, inspiring information you can begin to digest. You can read every book, including this one, go to every seminar, sign up for every retreat, but in the end you will have to be the one to rewrite the stories of your life. Meaning, you will have to be the one who dissolves the lies of unworthiness, not-good-enough-ness, I-can-only-have-this-ness, other-people-are-luckier-than-me-ness, things-will-never-work-out-ness, money-isn't-everything-ness, I-don't-care-ness, and recast it all with new beliefs full of love, beauty, grace, power, and abundance. And I tell you, it can be done. You can read about transformation, you can talk about transformation, you can produce talk shows about transformation, but only you can *be* transformed.

Moment by moment, day in and out, the world is reflecting back to you the stories you repeat to yourself on autopilot. You are the author and the storyteller and ultimately the experiencer of that creation, the good, the thrilling, the painful, and the downright awful. All of it.

At fifty-six years old, I found myself ready and willing to rewrite almost every single story of my life. And it will be, until the end of my days, a work in progress, but that intent and focus has taken my life in a wondrous new direction.

Here is an offering that you may find helpful: it's never too late to make the rest of your dreams come true.

And if not now, when?

The Beautiful No

1

If Not Now, When?

First we were so young and then we were so busy
and then one day we woke up to discover we
were at an age we once thought of as old.

—Anna Quindlen, *Lots of Candles, Plenty of Cake*

It's 8:30 in the morning, and I'm still in bed. Bella and Kissy, my English bulldogs, are snoring in unison. Outside, birds chirp in what sounds like an a cappella choral arrangement, interwoven with the far-off buzz of neighborhood lawn mowers. Haven't heard those sounds on a weekday in ages. I feel as if I've just woken up in another dimension.

Where am I?

Who am I?

What's happening?

The sun is up, morning has broken, and I have nowhere

to go. Nowhere to be. My calendar is empty for the first time in decades. The B-track whirrrrr of obligations, demands, responsibilities to others, and devotion to a mission I treated as my noblest calling, is echo-y silent. I'm not sure how I feel, but I do know this moment marks a categorically different phase of my life. Yesterday, after nearly twenty-one years of some of the most demanding producing work in television—the historic farewell season of *The Oprah Winfrey Show*, the stressful OWN turnaround, and the bittersweet closing of Harpo Studios in Chicago—I stood before the OWN staff and spoke for the last time as copresident.

"Today I am leaving OWN to make a dream I have had for a long time come true—to open a company of my own. What lights me up is storytelling, producing; that is where my heart is. Oprah, you put the world at my feet and opened the door to a spiritual life that makes this moment possible. Being with you day in, day out, these years, has been one big SuperSoul session. And to all of you, my colleagues from the beginning and those newer to the staff, thank you for being part of my wonderful life."

Our Los Angeles staff had gathered in my favorite space at OWN, the "magical café," full of light, pine, and potted trees, while the New York and Chicago staff joined in by videoconference. Oprah and I had shared my news with senior staff thirty minutes earlier. This speech was the final step before my departure. I felt calm and certain and centered. I had already shed my tears the night before while putting my parting words on paper. What a ride, what a journey, and now it was over. It was time to move on and tend to the whispers wafting in and around me that were getting louder and beginning to scream that my life needed serious tending to.

Yes, I was about to follow a new professional dream, as I told the gathered staff that day. But the truth is, that was only a small part of what was on my mind. Work has always driven the narrative of my life, so that piece was a no-brainer. It was a big bucket of personal life mess that was really calling my name. I am a true-blue, loyal-to-the-bone kind of person, and usually, it would take nothing short of a devastating betrayal to drive me away from someone or something to whom I have pledged my heartfelt devotion. And I had been devoted to my job for a very, very long time. But on a soul level, this transition felt ordained, as if the Universe was requiring my full and complete attention ASAP and there wasn't a second to lose.

I could see from the podium that my news caught people by surprise. When I finished, I soaked up the goodbyes, just for a few moments. Then Oprah and I headed to the elevator up to the offices one last time. Upstairs, I supervised some final packing, waved farewell, picked up my purse, and headed to my car.

The drive home felt like one of those big-deal life moments

that you generally don't recognize as such until much later. I knew I was supposed to be feeling something, but I didn't yet know what it was. I put down all the windows of my Range Rover, opened the sunroof, and had my own little Sheryl Crow moment as I took myself down iconic Santa Monica Boulevard—the drive to my house. Arriving home, I grabbed the phone, checked in with the people I love most, cuddled up with my puppies, put my feet up with a glass of wine, and went to bed early. As I drifted off to sleep my last thought was about what to do with this sense of "over-ness." But that would come later.

*   *   *

The next day I wake up to just me, the girls, the birds, and the empty space that used to be my schedule. It's day one of Life After Oprah.

I move through the morning in a cocoon. I feel numb. The world looks different without busyness to clutter and distract me. My brain is on pause. I have no feeling in my heart except a tiny little pilot-light flame of joy that I won't identify as such for several days. Quietly, I sip my coffee in my relatively new Los Angeles backyard.

I've lived in this house for just a few months, but already it feels like my sanctuary. From the first moment I laid eyes on the iron gate and splashing fountain inside, I knew something mystical had summoned me to her door. My realtor didn't have a planned appointment for this one on our home-tour agenda. I had scrolled through the Internet and noticed the listing. My assistant, Kim, heard me chatting about it and asked him to add it to our list. When I walked in the door, I knew. The house was a beauty: a Spanish colonial home built in 1926, in a neighborhood built on the former estate of the legendary Hollywood director Cecil B. DeMille. I spent months fixing her up with friends and famed designers Nate Berkus and Jeremiah Brent. Milky-white paint, French-gray shutters, copper lanterns, gray-and-white-striped awnings, three olive trees, six palm trees, eight pine trees, two jacarandas, boxwood hedges, climbing white roses, lusciously blooming hydrangeas, and espalier lemon trees. I had always lived in apartments and condos, so having my own "grounds" (midwestern translation: yard) was a milestone. I named her Belle Vie (French for *beautiful life*) the day I signed the contract, because new dreams for my life were beginning to stir.

Over the next few days, I stick close to this sanctuary of mine for some deep soul-searching. Slowly, I begin to probe the numbness, to let myself think the thoughts and ask the questions that will make my heart start to tingle and maybe even hurt a little.

No one would disagree that I've had the career of most people's dreams. Executive-producing the last five years of

The Oprah Winfrey Show was creative, demanding, fulfilling, and flat-out fun. I've also had the great good fortune to be part of a large, loving extended family and to have loyal friends whom I adore. Still, I haven't created magic all the way around for myself. Not even close. A few big dreams are yet to come true. I haven't created a truly beautiful life. My *belle vie*.

As I pour myself another cup of coffee, it is clear to me that I have a choice. At this moment, with my all-consuming career behind me, I can do one of two things. Option one: I can fully accept myself and my life the way it is right now, bid farewell to my inner critic, and firmly say "no, thank you" to the yearnings that sneak up on me in unguarded moments. Or option two: I can submit myself to a reckoning, a process of self-examination and reinvention so fierce and total that the walls I have so carefully constructed could come tumbling down for good. I feel a yearning to be brave.

* * *

Like most of us at this stage of the game, I am defined in many ways by the facts of my life.

I'm fifty-six years old. Single, no human children—but I count my beloved bulldogs as family members who seem to require as much care as toddlers. For my entire adult life, my career has been my everything. I don't blame my work for a moment, because it really was exactly what I wanted to do—it just so happened that for me, doing it well required a single-minded focus that left little time for anything else. Plus, there was so much to do I had the perfect excuse not to deal with any area of my life that didn't come quite so easily to me.

From the moment I grasped that bottom rung of the ladder as a lowly promo producer to the day I said farewell as co-president of the company, my double-decade stint working for Oprah was all-consuming. Still, I believe that even if I'd taken a different path, like gotten married, raised a family, *and* built a career, I'd be circling these same questions. Why do I default to making others' needs more important than my own? Why is my own well-being all too often the caboose on the train?

Fifty-six. When I say it out loud, it sounds older than I picture myself in my mind. A lot older. And it looks different on everyone, I notice. I'm not talking about gray hairs or wrinkles. When I glance around at women in my age range, I can see so clearly how we are each telling such different stories about what's possible for ourselves. You can tell by the way we move, by the way we talk, and the language we use; you can tell by the way we dress. You can tell by our energy, the smile in our eyes, or the listless exhausted stare of disappointment.

Some of us have clearly subscribed to the messages floating around in the ether, telling us that it's time to start winding the party down. "You've been to the ball and you had your chance to dance, you've made your bed and now there is nothing to do but lie in it and accept what life has doled out." In our culture, once women hit fifty-four years old and a day, nobody cares at all about what we think. The media industry actually stops tracking our opinions, viewing habits, and spending behavior. The twenty-five to fifty-four demographic, as it's known in the industry, is considered the advertising "sweet spot," which means anything outside that range is not worth targeting. Even though we fifty-five-plus people may finally have some money to spend or time to watch TV, they don't care. We're no longer relevant. At fifty-five years old, I ran a television network that, from a business perspective, could not have cared less about me. Oprah is older than I am. Imagine being the "name" of the network, the icon who founded it, and knowing they don't care about you either. Not one bit.

It's not just advertisers. All around us, the message is the same: you're done. Put on your stretchy pants and lace up your comfortable shoes; get a short, sensible wash-and-wear hairdo; and let the clock run out on your life while you wait for a chance to be useful to someone.

As I focus in on my new day, I find myself asking the same questions I know millions of other women are asking: Am I done now? Is what I have right now in my life all I get?

Here's the thing: I don't feel done. And here's some other breaking food for thought: the average life expectancy for the modern American woman is close to eighty. Who knows how far and how fast advances in medicine and technology may push the upper limits of our lives in the next few years? In this day and age, if you start taking care of yourself, it's not unreasonable to think that the fifties might truly be halfway up the mountain. This may be the middle of your life, not the beginning of the long goodbye. The actual *middle of your life* (not "midlife" as a kind euphemism for "old"). Once you take that in, really feel the expanse of time that offers you, maybe you'll start to feel a renewed energy. Maybe it's time to rethink *everything* about what is possible. Maybe it's time to dust off your dreams and give yourself permission to ask the "what about" question: *What about the life I always wanted?*

Here's what that means for me: What about the healthy fabulous body I had always wanted and never sustained? What about feeling at home in my own skin? What about unleashing my creativity and passion on my own projects for once? What about the deep, delicious soul-mate love that has eluded me? What about creating a more joy-filled life all the way around? It's hard to admit to myself that I still want these things, because right beneath those questions is a gnawing fear that I have left it too late.

Is this why so many of us stop dreaming at a certain stage of life? I wonder. It's all very well to entertain our longings when we're twenty-two and life is rolling out the red carpet of possibility before us (at least, that's how it looks in retrospect).

But by our fifties, dreaming feels fraught with uncomfortable emotions. We attempt to throw our imagination upstream but find ourselves swept back by the eddies of the past—the why-nots and what-ifs and WTFs. Our unfinished business seems to taunt us when we get too close to truth. So we try to shut it out with routine, smother it with layers of comfort and security, banish it with busyness, cheese, cocktails, or anything else that does the job.

I think maybe some put up a facade of contentment in midlife, because deep down they're afraid to say, "I want more." I want more than a roommate-like marriage as I roll downhill physically by piling on the pounds and not giving a shit. I want more than to guilt myself into spending time with people who drain the life out of me. I want more than to be somebody else's something. The real question is, are we brave enough to want our heart's desires? Are we daring enough to believe that we can have, be, or do what we want?

Are we?

Am I?

It takes courage to choose to dream rather than simply to continue down the same path. For many of us middle-of-lifers, we have thought and behaved our way into such big ruts that we don't even know we are stuck in them. We can't see how routinized our expectations have become. Or maybe we don't have the energy anymore to care about magic and potential and transformation. Creating a new vision of your life while you are smack-dab in the middle of it is a bold choice. Gathering up the courage to step out and think up new possibilities, having lived through decades of life, is very different from the wide-eyed dreams of a kid who hopes someday to become someone and do some big something.

On top of all that, there are generational beliefs that will challenge this wild idea that you get to have more of what you wanted for your life, now, in this middle time. When I was a little girl, I was admonished to take only one cookie from the plate when offered, even if I wanted to taste each kind. It was called being polite. That kind of early training gets translated in later years to "Don't take more than your share. You should be satisfied with what you have."

So we pretend that what we've conjured up so far is enough. We might even believe that our hands will be slapped back when we reach for a new helping at life's buffet. On some level, we rationalize it to ourselves: "You had the great career. You were well paid; you should be satisfied." Or "You have a beautiful family and a happy marriage; what more do you want?" Cha-ching, you're done. "You've got your health—that's more than many people can say. What are you complaining about?" You've had your serving at the table of abundance; you don't get to fill every cup.

I think about those messages and wonder what would

happen if I were to set them aside. What would happen if I were to begin to reframe the possibilities of my own life; to exercise my capacity to dream, now, in what I have decided is the middle of my life? Most important, what would happen if I set an intention to live each of those days with a reverence and appreciation I hadn't yet acquired and understood when I was younger and thought I would live forever?

Forever. Of course, none of us has endless time. We may indeed be in the middle of life and have more decades ahead than we've allowed ourselves to imagine. But it's equally true that every day could be our last, and therefore the life we've lived up until this moment is it. That's a bracing thought. As I let myself hold both these truths simultaneously—that I have so much more life to live *and* that this could be my last day on earth—I feel energized and also a little scared.

There is a sobering exercise many great teachers have used to get students to take stock of their lives. You are asked to visualize a graveyard and walk through the tombstones until you find your own. On the tombstone is one big headline, the lead story of your life. What does it say? I close my eyes and imagine I am walking toward an elegant little stone with a plaque in a pretty meadow. I read what I know in my heart is true:

SHERI SALATA.

SHE HAD A GREAT JOB. FOR A LONG TIME.

I've had a dream-come-true career but not a dream-come-true life. Will that be my whole story? What will be yours? Being someone's faithful wife, someone's excellent mother, or someone's devoted employee does not a full life make. It's not the whole dream. As I lift my eyes to the big, beautiful, expansive second half of life that is yet to be formed, I summon up the courage to take a good look at what I have created so far. It is time for a reckoning.

2

The Reckoning

Thursday morning.
One hundred pounds overweight, no man in sight,
and rounding the bend to 57 years old—a full-blown
catastrophe.

—From a Post-it note, written by me, May 2016

The good news about the middle of life is that you may have thirty, forty, even fifty years ahead of you. The not-always-so-good news is that you've also got that many years and maybe more behind you. You're not starting out with a clean slate. No, ma'am. By the time you hit fifty, you've been through some shit. You've been disappointed, disenchanted, betrayed, and brokenhearted. You may feel worn out and wonder if you can even summon up the gumption and the energy for a middle-of-life reinvention. After all, you've probably done your share of those, too: the diet plans; the new workout regimens; the thirty days of this, that, or the other thing.

I can relate. I've tried working with trainers, spinning, running half marathons. High-protein diets, low-fat diets, packages of processed diet food. (And by the way, they all work until you end the program . . . and then you pile the pounds back on.) I've done as many do-overs as there are Mondays. I don't have the energy for another one either. The revisioning I'm talking about is something deeper than all of those. It's sitting quietly with my failures, my slipups, my undealt-with anger, my unacknowledged hurt. I need to understand where I'm starting from.

Can you tenderly look at the landscape of your life and lovingly explore its pits and grooves, its highs and lows, without unleashing the harsh, hateful, and truly mean voice that lives inside your head? You know that voice all too well. It's the tape that plays over and over that you barely notice but that rules your universe. You are too this, too that, not enough this, not enough that. Can you quiet that voice and find the sweet, loving part of you that has been there for all of your friends, holding the light in the midst of their most devastating failures and worst mistakes? Can you just this once be *that* for yourself? The process of reinventing yourself and revisioning your life requires not only courage but a deep sense of compassion we don't ordinarily shine on ourselves. It's brave to look at what you've created in every area of your life, and the compassion keeps you from wanting to resist the painful parts. It's the reckoning that launches the dream. And it's a necessary part of the process that can't be shortchanged.

Are you strong enough to look with fresh eyes at the story of your life? To read what you've written so far? That means what works. What doesn't. What is life-giving. What is soul-sapping. It's the big spring cleaning of your life: sweeping under the beds, clearing out the closets. Shaking up the energy and getting things moving. It is the unearthing of what your heart desires now—not what you thought you wanted thirty years ago, but now. It is the beginning of the upward spiral where it feels like the universe exists to delight and surprise you with wonder. But only after you dig in and do a Marie Kondo–like tidying-up, keeping only what you truly love and getting rid of everything else.

I've executive-produced enough makeover shows to know you can't jump straight to the happy ending, the "after" photo. What makes the transformation meaningful is the "before." And the great stories don't just leap from before to after, they weave a narrative that connects the struggles to the triumphs, the despair to the elation. The same is true for your story. If you want to write the kind of ending that you hardly dare to imagine, you first need to find the courage to own your own beginnings and middles. All of them. And there's no time to waste.

I have reframed my view of my own life, realizing that I have a whole second half to create. But I also understand that on a quantum level, all I have is today. This day. And I have squandered more than my share of "this days" on things that didn't matter to me, worries that never materialized, people-pleasing that yielded nothing but my own resentment. I know in every cell of my being that I want to live the life of my dreams, and I know that it must begin with a real reckoning: an honest-to-goodness, bone-crunching, gut-wrenching rebuild; a true change of heart. Body, mind, and spirit, along with romantic love, career, family, and friends—all of it. Nothing else will be enough.

* * *

I start where I know it will hurt. My body.

I am one hundred pounds overweight. Not ten, not thirty, not all the other weights I was overweight. Now, I am one hundred pounds overweight. For years I've have played that game: How many pounds overweight would be really, really, really bad? I passed that point a while back. And kept going.

A person who has not had weight issues may struggle to understand how you can make yourself unconscious about how fat you are as you continue to dial up the fast-food delivery orders for comfort, for relieving stress, for feeling less lonely, or for any other old reason you can conjure up. But you can. And what's more, you can make it clear, energetically, to everyone around you that you have no wish to discuss it, so that everyone who cares about you knows this topic is taboo. You stop looking in mirrors and start collecting a wardrobe of indistinguishable *schmattas* (big, black blousy things) in which you can face the world, erroneously believing you have hidden the pounds from public view. Then you literally don't think about it. Ever.

P.S. That also means you must banish anything connected to your body from your life (i.e., sex, fashion, swimming in an actual bathing suit and not a "swimming costume," and pretty much anything else that requires feeling good in your own skin).

Now, in the solitude of my room, I force myself to turn toward the source of my discomfort. It's time, I remind myself. Time to ask the questions I've not allowed anyone to ask me, including myself. What is this about, this weight? The ups and downs over decades?

The last sixty-five pounds aren't a huge mystery. I have dealt with a heaping plateful of the good and the bad these past seven years, and I'm still standing. The sudden death of my younger brother, John, at the age of forty-four; the heart-crushing worry for his widow and four little children;

my mother's heroic five-year journey with stage four cancer; executive-producing *The Oprah Winfrey Show* for five seasons, through the twenty-fifth farewell year; conquering a full-blown smoking addiction; the metabolic slowdown of turning fifty; the strain of the OWN cable channel turnaround with its bi-coastal demands; packing up everything I owned and moving to California after almost thirty years in Chicago; and (most worth looking at, I think) a deeply rooted lack of self-love.

I pause and exhale, realizing that I've been holding my breath as this stream of truth pours out onto the page. Don't try to fix it, I tell myself. Just keep looking.

My health. This weight has created real issues, beginning with the fact that I haven't moved much in a year. I can't haul myself up on a SoulCycle bike anymore, can't run without injuring my knees, and, besides, some days a workout is just asking too much, emotionally. It's as if my body has been programmed to conserve all energy just to get through what must be done, and those things don't have much to do with me and my well-being. Last but not least, and certainly not surprising, my cholesterol is high, and I have all the markers of inflammation. Aging well, biologically, I'm not.

I take a deep breath and put down my notebook. It's so tempting to jump to solutions—to start googling diets and health clubs, or ordering the latest fitness equipment online. But I'm not doing that. I refuse to go down those roads again.

I step out onto the balcony and stretch, as the sun sinks low on the horizon. Bella and Kissy need to be walked. I'm raw from steeping myself in what I've held at bay for years. That's enough reckoning for one day.

*   *   *

My true feelings about my body were a hard one for me, but that's why it was the right place to start. The reckoning becomes real when you seek out the most raw, vulnerable corners of your life; the ones you'd do anything to avoid looking at. For you, that starting place might be something else entirely. Perhaps your money situation is a scary mess and you need to reckon with a pile of debt or an insecure future. Perhaps your family life is in tatters. Perhaps you're stuck in a job that you're afraid to admit is suffocating your soul. Remember to have compassion for yourself as you begin to look. And when you're done, move on to another area of life. Some will be hard; others will be easier.

Item number two on my list is one that I'm much more comfortable looking at. Spirituality. This is one area of my life that I made a priority years ago, and it continues to be a focus. As I reflect on my journey, I see how I have expanded my thinking and connected to my inner being—my soul—more deeply over time. In fact, it's a reason why, in the midst of this gut-wrenching self-examination, I am not in a heap on the floor.

Raised Catholic and lapsing in my college years, I found the beginning of a real spiritual life thanks to my job at *The Oprah Winfrey Show*. It was so much more than a career; it was my doorway to connection to the All of All, the Universe, a higher power. Oprah introduced me to new ideas, new practices, and some of the foremost spiritual masters of our time. I devoured all of Oprah's recommended books, and I got to meet the authors in person. They awakened a spiritual language that resonated with me and eventually led me to the spiritual teachers known as Abraham-Hicks. I stumbled upon their teachings late one night while surfing the Web, and they spoke to me like none other. I felt like I'd gone straight to the Source. So simple, yet so true, these teachings resonated in every cell.

Now, as part of my reckoning, I write down in my notebook the essence of what I've learned:

We cocreate our reality with the Universe.
We are responsible for it all.
Ask.
It is given.
Allow it.

I must pay attention to my thoughts, my feelings, and my words, because through them I am "calling in" my next experience in every moment. And what a life I have called in! I've been the chief architect of so much wonder and abundance. And yes, I've also been the creator of heartbreak and emptiness. I have manifested the best and the worst, and I am living it, simultaneously, right now. I did it, all of it. And I am doing it, each and every day.

Which brings me, reluctantly, to the next item on my list.

* * *

Love.

Specifically, sexy, romantic, passionate, real soul-to-soul love.

This is tough. Embarrassing. And tinged with what feels like genuine shame.

Love is my unsolved mystery—one of the great enigmas of my life. Why does something that appears to be like breathing to others feel like Cirque du Soleil to me? I see a couple strolling along, hand in hand, clearly in love, and my reaction is: beautiful to look at but impossible to pull off myself.

It's been years since I walled off the part of me that yearns for love. Other than crushes and flings and affairs, I've used a million "I'm too busy" excuses to avoid the real deal. Why? To protect myself from disappointment and hurt? Yes, that's part of it. But there is something even more fundamental. I'm not sure what it is yet. But I think I'm ready to find out.

I'm about to close my notebook and take a break when a memory sneaks up on me, uninvited. It's 2012, and I'm sitting in an arena with several thousand others. Oprah is sitting beside me, listening with rapt attention as Tony Robbins works his magic on the attendees at his Unleash the Power Within seminar. All day, we've been captivated as he has paced the stage with almost supernatural energy and ventured out into the crowd, delivering powerful, life-changing messages and on-the-spot coaching to those audience members who dared to stand up and reveal their most intimate secrets. I found myself gasping at the bravery of these people, even as my stomach churned for them, and I made sure to keep my hands tightly in my lap so it would not appear, under any circumstances, that I wanted to join in.

Now, Tony has left the stage again and is making his way through the crowd. He begins to tell a story that sounds vaguely familiar, about a woman who's shut herself off from love because she believes she isn't "good" at it. "Rather than open herself to love," he says, "this woman chose instead to focus on her career because she knew how to shine there— how to get an A-plus."

Tony is slowly, theatrically, ascending the steps below where we're sitting, continuing his story as he goes. "Until she is willing to get in the ring and take some big risks, this woman is never going to have the life she's dreamed of," he declares. And then he looks up, and our eyes lock. He continues looking at me. I freeze in my seat.

"Oh my God. He's talking about me and he's coming over here and he's gonna call on me," I whisper to Oprah in a panic.

"He wouldn't do that," she reassures me. After all, we're not just any old seminar participants. We're here preparing for Oprah's upcoming interview with Tony. I allow myself to relax for a moment.

Then Oprah takes another look at Tony and shakes her head. "No, you're right. He's coming right for you."

And he does. He walks right up to our row—and keeps walking. Oprah and I double over, rocking back and forth in silent hysterics. She, because it was really funny; me, with crazed relief. But I know I wasn't wrong. I just think that as a world-renowned expert on human behavior, Tony no doubt realized I would have had some sort of psychological collapse if he had stopped at my chair, so he walked on by.

The next day, when Oprah asked him, Tony confirmed what I already knew. He'd been speaking directly to me— the girl, now woman, who hates to fail. He saw, more clearly than anyone ever had, one of the traits that forms the barrier between me and romantic love.

I sit with that memory. It doesn't feel good. It doesn't feel good to still be single at fifty-six, and to know that the real reason is that I was too afraid. Not too busy, too successful, too heavy, too tired. I denied myself love because I didn't want to fail. But as I allow those feelings to wash over me, I become aware that there's another feeling, too—a faint glow of something that might just be called excitement if I could turn up its volume about a hundred times.

I focus on that feeling, and I start to remember the times I've felt like I've been in love. I can feel how my heart leaped when he called or put his hand possessively on the small of my back. I recall how perfect life felt when he threw a passionate glance across a crowded room, or we spent a lazy Sunday morning together, shutting out the world. These beautiful memories are part of the reckoning, too—I've been holding them at bay as fiercely as I've shut out my shame and self-criticism. Now, I let myself remember how life is so much more delicious when you participate in the dance—when you say yes to love with joie de vivre. The glow gets brighter. I think that maybe, after all these years, I am ready to lower the drawbridge and let love in.

*   *   *

Reckoning has a rhythm. The stories that have shaped us don't come to the surface all at once. As you make space for your own truth, from the dark to the light, be sensitive to those moments when you need to rest, to rejuvenate, to simply be. This is not a "beat yourself up party" as you stridently laundry-list all the comprehensive evidence of your inherent unworthiness to an imaginary judge and jury. That behavior needs to be lovingly vacated. This is about laying the foundation for your new beginning, launching a quest that will lead you to joy and peace and real love.

I slept deeply last night, as if exhausted by the emotional exertion of it all. This morning, I'm ready to move down the list.

Family and friends. In this category I give my life high marks—I am crazy about my family. The Polish-Lithuanian Salatas, with nine first cousins, are like the von Trapp family from *The Sound of Music*—a singing, dancing gang of pure joy. "Edelweiss" is our three-part harmonic clarion call. Each new generation is as delightful as the one that came before, and without fail each December we gather on the Saturday night before Christmas to bask in the glow of sauerkraut and noodles.

My mom's side of the family is smaller but equally wonderful. I spent countless Saturdays at Gram's kitchen table with my little cousins, Christine and Cathy, listening to the Swedish-Scots-Irish Anderson girls, my mom and her best friend and older sister, Donna, chat it up as they drank pots of Folgers, sipped on Coca-Colas, and smoked cigarettes.

My brother, John, and I, and everyone on both sides of my family, were raised to care for one another, which is the legacy of the matriarchs who ruled the world we knew—our grandmothers, Annie and Julia. They were working moms who stretched a dime, made sure their children had better than they had, and insisted that their grandchildren gather on a regular basis. They had a reverence for tradition. Family was not just important; family was everything. I am the reflection of both of my grandmothers: a working girl who relishes ceremony just like they taught me. I believe that in the ways that count, I have grown to embody the best of them.

Regarding friends, I am drawn to salt-of-the-earth types. Most friends I've known for decades, and we are "have your back no matter what" loyal to each other. These are relationships rooted in commingled hopes, dreams, and sorrows over thousands of days and tens of thousands of heart-to-hearts. Marriages. Divorces. Babies. Jobs. Puppies. Moves. Triumphs. Disasters. And lots of cocktails.

My newer friends are a revelation to me. They have shown up in surprising diversity, age-wise, from much younger to older. I am fascinated by how this fills my cup with new perspectives and fresh energy. I, who had a firm belief that I had all the friends I needed, have done a complete turnaround. Bring them on, I say. This new and old friendship brew is turning out to be an excellent mix, and I can feel myself expanding with each conversation and encounter.

Still, this reckoning would not be complete if I didn't get down-to-the-bone honest here, too. The truth is, I have a pathological aversion to personal conflict. I hate it and will go to the ends of the earth to avoid it. This has allowed me to tolerate all kinds of poor treatment, just to keep the peace. For so many years, I have done the thing I thought I should do, in order to make people happy. I have shown up when I didn't really want to, out of obligation and self-imposed guilt. I have apologized repeatedly, for no reason at all, to keep an old connection afloat. I have relentlessly excused thoughtless, unloving behavior and passive-aggressive energy long after it was time to let go. And that pattern must end.

I want to be loosed of relationships that no longer serve me. And with this comes an increasing desire, pounding in my heart like a drumbeat, to only do what I want to do, when I want to do it, and with whom I wish to do it. I am not interested in tearing apart others, commiserating over fear and failure (at least, no more than five minutes max), or revisiting tired territory that should have been abandoned years ago. I am tending to my own stuff, and my wish is that everyone in my life do the same. Insecurities, jealousies, and a thousand and one excuses for why someone cannot make better choices is a stew I will simmer in no more. And if you are deceitful or disloyal, then there will be nothing for us to share.

I want to revel in possibilities. I want to laugh and dance and sing and drink great wine and celebrate and love and discuss the Universe and all its magic.

My bar has just been raised.

It's a new day.

*   *   *

The last item on my list is a topic that once consumed my days. In fact, I was obsessive and singularly focused—a "work comes first" kind of gal.

Now, that W-word can be an awful trigger for me. My pulse will race, my blood will rise up, and I will suddenly be flooded with thoughts that I need to be doing something other than exactly what I'm doing right now. I'll feel convinced that whatever stillness or space I might be experiencing will need to be filled up, or those proverbial balls in the air will be tumbling down right on my head. Keep moving. Don't sit down. Stay vigilant.

Let me just be clear that I feel nothing but appreciation for the professional opportunities that came my way for so many years. Career-wise, I won the megabucks life lottery. And I gave it my all. My midwestern sense of commitment to doing my duty came before everything but a downright personal crisis, family illness, or catastrophe. It's how I rolled, how I believed I was "built."

The truth was, however, that work became my go-to excuse for avoiding all the areas of life that were more challenging for me. "I have to w—." "I have so much w— to do." And let's not even get started on the B-word. "She's sooooo busy" was how I was described by anyone who knew me. But not once in all that time did anyone ever question or challenge my choices. I was "too busy" working for the most famous woman in the world, on one of the most successful shows in TV history. It was an awesome career, and no one could disagree with that.

But as I examine it now, clearly my life was ruled by a misguided belief that my absolute value and worth as a human being was directly tied to achievement. To getting the gold star. I alone wasn't enough.

In this next professional phase, I want to work for myself. I imagine having the freedom to set my own schedule, to see possibilities to be pursued rather than problems to be solved. Far fewer "to do" lists. Far more "to be" lists. And consequently, far less doing, far more being. Most of all, I dream of having my work in the world be integrated into the rest of my life.

One life.

Not a work life and a personal life, like drawers in a desk. One life, where my areas of interest, the things that matter to me, what gives meaning to my life meld together and intersect with one another. Where I choose my priorities. Where taking a walk with my girls, Bella and Kissy, is as vital as delivering on a deadline because that's my new standard.

*　　*　　*

My reckoning takes several days. Days during which I barely leave the house. Some moments I just feel angry and disgusted with myself. How could I have treated myself so poorly? Other moments, it worsens to shame and contempt. When I'm finished, I feel sick at heart, unbearably sad, and awash in what I think is regret.

The bottom line is this: I have been an untrustworthy steward of my own well-being.

And that's when I can feel rock bottom under my feet. I reread my Post-it note where I jotted down the state of my life.

Thursday morning. One hundred pounds overweight, no man in sight, and rounding the bend to 57 years old—a full-blown catastrophe.

It's a humiliating description for a woman who had a seat at some of the most leading-edge personal-development conversations ever, who met some of the most prolific thought leaders and spiritual teachers on the planet. Who had notebooks filled with every little nugget that gave her an aha moment. Who ran half marathons, scaled mountains, was trained to meditate, and immersed herself in spiritual workshops and reading as if her life depended on it. I had more information than most, could recite the tenets of best-life living backward and forward. I'd produced stadium tours entirely devoted to those ideas. In fact, I could produce the hell out of transformation. I just continued to avoid producing the transformation of my own life.

Surprisingly, my mood shifts. Instead of contempt, I reach for tenderness, a deep, deep tenderness that has been absent from my internal voice since I can remember. What I have uncovered is my unlived life. *My unlived life.* I recognize this as the grand epiphany of my reckoning. It pulsates with an energy that feels sacred and true. My unlived life—a spare and powerful truth that can set me free. And if I will summon my own capacity for compassion and direct it toward myself, as a new practice, I can begin again and learn to inhabit every square inch of it.

In the end, the reckoning—my reckoning, your reckoning—is not about self-judgment. It's about hope. It's the beginning of the stirring up of possibility. It's the seed of the tiniest momentum that propels you beyond the ruts you are stuck in, the routine you have so dedicatedly constructed over decades. Yes, it can be painful to consider the past, the missed chances, the wasted time, because it confronts us with what might have been. But once you have examined your unlived life, you hold in your hand the map to your dreams.

The next stop on my map is deep in the Mojave Desert.

3

My Pink Life

We are the most beautiful, intricate, gloriously accurate instruments of this universe. I stand in reverence before the wisdom of every cell of my body, and I would never do anything to abuse or injure it.

—Susana Belen, health and wellness pioneer

Weeks after my dramatic middle-of-life reckoning, on a blue-sky Sunday afternoon, I find myself in the middle of the desert, losing my shit. Literally.

I've come to Desert Hot Springs, about two hours east of Los Angeles, for an eight-day supervised fast at We Care, a much-heralded health and wellness center whose signature detox protocol includes daily colonics. Yes, you read that right. The centerpiece of the We Care experience is a treatment called colon hydrotherapy, otherwise known as a good old-fashioned enema (though with much more sophisticated equipment than the bucket and a rubber hose that your grandmother might have had in her bathroom cabinet). Some doctors think it's a bunch of malarkey, while others say it is a key ingredient to good digestive health, aka "gut health." I say to each his own. I am willing to try it.

In many ways, this trip is the formal kickoff to what I am coming to realize is a lifesaving mission. It will be part one of a personalized intervention that I will create, step-by-step, to reclaim my well-being and begin to evolve my life. After years of neglect, I am willing to make this reclamation project my absolute unflinching priority—to nourish, rejuvenate, and heal the body I inhabit. I want more than information, though; I have enough information to carry me through eternity. I want to be blessed.

I think we all need to be blessed. For many of us at this stage of the life game, we've dashed our own hopes so many times that we eye our own intentions with a spirit-killing dose of skepticism. We just don't believe anymore that we can have that *ta-da* happy ending. We've let ourselves down one too many times. We feel we don't deserve our own trust. And maybe on some deep, deep level—the level that is private and off-limits to all—we are protecting our hearts from an acknowledgment of personal failing that will be so searing in its pain we would rather march on down the road to the end of our days and avoid the whole kit and caboodle. Pretend like we never wanted more. Pretend like it doesn't matter anyway. Pretend. Avoid. Block. Numb.

Besides the serious physical protocol that We Care offers, I am here because, for the first time in what feels like forever, I desperately need to put together a string of days with no in-box emergencies. I need time with no phone calls, no wall-to-wall meetings, and no underlying sense of guilt for not being on duty and at the ready. I need a peace I haven't allowed myself for years.

We Care is one of those whispered, Hollywood-insider kinds of secrets. It has been rumored that many big stars have come here to prepare their bodies for roles that required a shocking physical transformation. The people I know who tout its virtues are the type who are serious about their physical well-being. They aren't playing around. The founder, Susana Belen, an eighty-year-old spark plug originally from Argentina, is considered one of the pioneers in detoxification and extreme wellness. Now her daughter Susan runs their acclaimed program. When I got lucky because of a last-minute cancellation, I knew it was fate intervening. I drove the two and a half hours from Los Angeles early on a Sunday morning and arrived feeling world-weary, like a saggy helium balloon three days after the party.

Leading up to my departure, I had done five days of

prescribed preparation that involved no caffeine, alcohol, sugar, or anything starchy—basically, just green vegetables and fruit. With the prep over it was time for the actual fast. I was apprehensive about not eating solid food for eight days, which seemed like a really long time. There would also be yoga, a lot of wellness classes, massages and treatments to encourage more detoxification, infrared saunas and a pool (which I would gaze at longingly as I wilted in the crackling heat, but never enter due to ongoing body shame), and, of course, the daily colonics.

When I first pulled up to the gates, the radiant light that turned the surrounding mountains purply-orange made me gasp. I had a fleeting memory that I'd always claimed I wasn't a desert person. I wondered why I said that. This was beautiful in a deeply soulful way. The hacienda-like structure wasn't slick or intimidating but more like a super-lived-in cozy home. I liked it immediately. The main house sat around the sweet kidney-shaped pool. Desert garden paths led to various treatment rooms and guest villas. The friendly vibe belied the power of the place, as I would find out soon enough. At the time, We Care could only accommodate seventeen people, which suited me just fine. I didn't really want much interaction. I needed to be alone.

*   *   *

If I've been worried about what I will do with myself over these next several days, my fears are quickly allayed. From dawn to dusk, I'll be preparing a myriad of different teas, elixirs, and blended vegetable soups. In all, I'll be imbibing about fourteen drinks per day, along with as much alkaline lemon water as I can get down. There are also special supplements, including green food, fiber, enzymes, and probiotics. I must admit, I love a program, and I have put myself on a serious one by coming to We Care. I have a sneaking suspicion, though, that I am going to feel worse before I feel better. Detoxing from sugar, salt, alcohol, caffeine, and animal products is often accompanied by headaches, exhaustion, and an overall feeling of yuck that can last for several days while you are clearing things out.

From a spiritual perspective, the ritual that sets the stage for real transformation is the first-night fire ceremony. Mari, a trained shaman of many lineages and a master healer, leads us in a writing exercise designed to help us each uncover what we want to leave in the desert: a shedding of situations, people, events, and beliefs that no longer serve us or our greatest happiness. She passes out feather-like pens in bright colors and scrolls of paper. We all sit around the circle and work on our lists intently. I can hear tiny sobs around me. As I look over my list, I see much of the reckoning I have just done back in Los Angeles reflected on my paper here. Every area of my life I have examined so carefully. So much to let go of.

lavender. It smells like heaven and takes me to what feels like an alternate reality.

She demonstrates what we came here to do, taking her own list of things that no longer serve her, walking around the fire pit, and then placing it inside the cauldron. I watch as the smoke from her list rises toward the sky, and I can almost see her words dissolve in the air. One by one, each person follows her example, and again and again, the smoke carries those private aches and pains to another realm—gone like a wisp on the wind.

The sun is setting and the desert night air is beginning to chill as I stand up with my scroll in hand and walk toward the fire. I hold my list to my lips and whisper a sincere prayer of farewell to all of it, and then I lean down and place it in the dancing flames. The list sparks, crackles, and then becomes a rising gray smoke of transcendence. The ceremony is complete and my releasing is done. I walk off by myself and weep a little. I am feeling especially tender and raw. The sun is gone, and now that I have symbolically let go of so much, I wonder what is next for me.

*   *   *

The week continues with its daily self-care routine, and I follow it meticulously. I am detoxing, of course, and that looks like sleeping ten hours a night and needing a nap or two to get through the day. But to my amazement I am never hungry. How can that be? The centerpiece of the program is the daily colonic, and the experience does not disappoint.

Here is what happens when you take the plunge. You climb on a table and lie on your side. A tube is inserted that will deliver gallons of water to your colon. A trained colon hydrotherapist massages your tummy with warm oil as the "filling" and "emptying" continues for about forty-five minutes. You can watch the carnage, and it is something to see—especially when you haven't eaten solid food in a week. I feel like I am dropping major pounds by the minute—an added bonus.

"Hypnotherapy for Weight Loss." The brochure is pinned to the bulletin board in the main gathering room. This optional private class immediately piques my interest, and I sign up for the three-session package. I've never been hypnotized, and I figure it can't hurt at this point. At the appointed time, there is a knock on the door of my villa, and in comes an elegant, lovely woman who is clearly in fabulous shape. (I would learn later she looks much younger than she is.) Renee Cardenas is a clinical hypnotherapist who grew up in Argentina and immigrated to the States, where she established a thriving practice in Los Angeles. Ready for a new experience, she then headed east to Desert Hot Springs and joined the We Care staff as a healer.

I've signed up for these sessions in part to keep myself busy while I await my next detox drink and colonic, but I am hoping, just a little, that Renee will turn out to be skilled enough to help prod a breakthrough for me. She will need to have some serious game, however. I have been to the mountaintop of experts in human behavior and transformation and have heard the best of the best. It's a high bar for her to clear. I also hope that I will be smart enough to allow myself to be helped. Bring it on, I think, as Renee sets up for the session. I am ready to tackle my weight issue with hypnosis. But right off the bat, things take a different turn.

"Why are you here?" she asks.

I tell her I have conducted a comprehensive reckoning with myself, and, clearly, I want to lose weight. I tell her that this time it has really gotten away from me, even more than the other times. I don't get the sense that Renee is super-impressed with all the soul-searching I've done over the past several weeks. She isn't willing to skip the formalities and move on to the magical process I am expecting.

"Give me a detailed account of your weight history."

I sigh. When are we going to get to the good stuff? Let the hypnotizing commence already.

I know this narrative by heart, and the last thing I want to do is tell it again. But I take a deep breath and begin.

I was about ten years old and sitting in the office of

Dr. Kostalek, my pediatrician. She said to my naturally skinny mother, "You are going to have to watch her weight. Sheri is going to have a tendency to gain more than she should." I was in fourth grade and weighed sixty-six pounds. For my height, I wasn't fat, or even chubby, but in short order the famed zero-calorie cabbage soup diet and sugar-free Fannie May candies for diabetics became my daily fare. The seed was planted. I was the "fat" one in the family. My mom, who honestly didn't know she was making things worse, would eyeball my body up and down on a daily basis to see if the good doctor's prophecy was coming true. It made me want to sneak off and inhale a box of Twinkies.

Cheerleading and tennis kept me in shape through my teens, and from there I held pretty steady until after college. Then came the stress of earning my own living in a series of crazy jobs. I was also partying up a storm and eating cheap cheesy carbs from dawn to dusk. I became an emotional eater, stuffing down any pressure I was feeling, celebrating, comforting myself, you name it—every emotion on the spectrum applied. Between the ages of twenty-five and fifty-five, I became the poster girl for weight-loss systems. From Diet Center (twice) to Atkins (untold attempts), from Jenny Craig (thrice) to South Beach, Blood Type Diet, and more, I lost and gained the same twenty to twenty-five pounds more times than I could count.

Gradually, the weight swing rose to between forty and sixty pounds.

During the *Oprah Winfrey Show* years, I joined in with every fitness movement we produced for viewers, trained for the San Diego half marathon with fellow staffers, and did the thirty-day vegan challenge. I couldn't hold any success I achieved for long. I had a deeply honed pattern that once I hit my goal, or got close, I was done and the deprivation could cease. Let the celebration begin. So, for decades, I played the feast-or-famine diet game. On then off. Fat then skinny then fat again.

My eating habits as a television talk-show executive producer were disastrous. Sixteen-hour days were not uncommon, and fast food was my sustenance. Venti skim lattes all day long. Jumbo Diet Cokes for hydration. Fried-egg sandwiches at 6:00 a.m., Subway clubs, Cobb salads smothered in blue cheese dressing, Italian beef sandwiches, turkey Reubens, and frozen pizzas at home, with chips-and-dip appetizers. I had no desire to spend my precious free hours outside of work cooking. I went out or ordered in. That became a way of life that eventually led to this chair across from Renee, in the middle of the Mojave Desert.

I glance up at her and notice she is listening closely.

"I brought something for you," she says, and puts some

paper and colored markers on the table in front of me. I groan inwardly. I hate this kind of thing.

"I want you to draw a picture of yourself today. Don't think about it, just draw," she instructs. "Then I want you to draw another picture, of yourself as you dream of being."

This is starting to feel like how I imagine "therapy" feels. Nearly everyone I know has been in therapy. Except me. I dipped my toe in the pond when I was twenty-eight years old, working as a secretary at an ad agency and living in downtown Chicago. I had little money, and the therapist who saw several of my coworkers was willing to do a sliding scale. Turns out you get what you pay for, and my $35 didn't go far. At 5:30 (the soonest I could get to her office after work) she would have me lie on her couch, and we'd begin our one-hour session. By her side was one of those Optifast miracle-weight-loss shakes popular in the eighties, which should have tipped me off she didn't totally have it together herself. Ten minutes into the session, she would stop talking and begin to snore. I'd lie on the couch and stare at the ceiling as the hour ticked by. At the five-minutes-left mark, I'd wake her up with a throat clearing and a couple coughs, and she would act as though nothing out of the ordinary had happened. I saw her only three times. I never had the heart to tell her she had slept through our therapy. (What does it say about my then-shaky self-esteem that I worried more about her embarrassment than her neglect of me?) That was my first and last time exploring my subconscious in therapy.

I look at Renee without speaking, just long enough to wordlessly convey that I think this arts-and-crafts exercise is borderline silly. Then I pick up the marker and begin to draw the way I see myself at this moment, and then the person I dream of being. I do it. Just to move us along.

"Look at these pictures side by side," she says, "and tell me what you see."

What I see leaves me stunned. In the first drawing is a stick figure with a swoosh of blond hair. Where the eyes should be are two blue *X*s and where the mouth should be is a big red *X*. I've drawn a blind, mute version of me. A worn-out woman who is unwilling to see what is happening to her and doesn't speak about what is happening to her. Deliberate unconsciousness. Deliberate oblivion. I feel sick as I describe her to Renee.

The second drawing features the same stick figure, but this version is kind of sparkly, in a swingy feminine dress (or as best I could approximate one with my markers). Her eyes are blue and open and flirty, and she has lipstick-smiley lips and outstretched arms. Even in my amateurish marker drawing, her energy for life is palpable and her magic is big. I stare at the sheet of paper longingly.

Renee brings me back to the moment by asking me to choose another marker and giving me a third sheet of paper.

"Now," she says, "draw what needs to happen for the woman in the first picture to become the woman in the second picture."

I suppress any thinking, as instructed, and just start drawing. When I am done, what I see on the page is a door frame with an open door swinging away to "somewhere out there." On either side of the door frame, at the bottom, there are flower beds and some fringy grass. On the right-hand side there is a little wooden sign planted in the grass that simply says: "Now, just walk through." Stars twinkle in the sky above.

Could it possibly be that simple? After we wrap our session for the day, I sit with the drawings in front of me for hours. On these papers is the incontrovertible evidence. How my subconscious sees me now. Who I want to be. How to get there.

I spend the rest of the day thinking about what lies on the other side of my hand-drawn door.

I wonder how many other women my age are staring at the same doorway? Are they, too, wondering how to walk through? To new outcomes, new dreams for their lives? No matter what we've lived through, no matter how badly we have fucked it all up or allowed our lives to wither into near oblivion, do we each in some way carry the tiniest seed of hope that there might be more? That we might have one more chance at real, sustainable joy? It is said that when you make the smallest change in the present, the entire trajectory of your life is dramatically altered. There is mathematical hope in that equation alone. My eyes land again on my drawing of that door—the very simple, elegant message from my subconscious. In my mind, again, I think of "my tribe"—all those strangers in the same boat—and what the symbolism might mean for all of us. I have a sense that the doorway details might be different for everyone but that the essence is fundamentally and universally shared. And that essence has to do with love.

The next day's session brings up new things to consider. Renee starts with a meditation that requires me to look behind me and imagine the trail of my past—the awesome and the ugly. She has me literally stand up, close my eyes, and twist around so my closed eyes are aimed behind me, looking at the decades of time that have brought me to this moment. Once I have taken that in and really felt the full roller-coaster terrain of that past, Renee ends our time together with a provocative question. "That is the past. None of it is real anymore. Not even the glorious stuff. Not even the top-of-the-mountain career stuff. Are you willing to let go of all of it and walk through the new door you drew yesterday?"

She leaves me in my room somewhat dazed and promises to see me the next day.

In our final session, Renee and I talk about what is on the other side of the door. I tell her I've been formulating a theory that my way through that metaphoric portal will be to customize a way of living that is totally personal to me. No more diet plans. No more one-size-fits-all. No more deprivation or stringent protocols designed by others for a mass market. I have decided to take my producer skills and enlist them in service to my own happiness—to create my own recipe and then tweak it regularly like an alchemist. A pinch of this. A pinch of that. More of what feels good, less of what doesn't. In all areas. Food, workout, spirituality, friends, family, love, creativity—all of it.

And the big key, I realize, will be setting down the false sense that I have to hold the world up with my two bare hands. *I am in charge of nothing and no one but myself. That is where my power lies.* Even as I say these words to Renee, I know in my soul that I have finally linked up with the "being" piece of creating the life of my dreams—the piece that has eluded me in all my years of "doing."

When I finish, Renee is smiling. "That sounds like a good life, Sheri. Let me ask you something. This new life you're formulating for yourself, can you put a color to it?"

Strangely, I can put a color to it, as I sit in my air-conditioned We Care room that June day, swathed in black from head to toe. "It's pink. Like the desert sky. It's a pink life I'm creating."

"Open your hand and close your eyes," she says. "I picked this up on the grounds on my way over to see you today." She places something cool and hard on my palm. I open my eyes and there I see a small pink rock. We smile at each other. She doesn't need to tell me to anchor my dreams to this rock; I know that's what it's for.

After a few more days, more colonics, and long walking meditations in the pink light of the desert—while holding my pink rock—I break my fast with a small vanilla protein smoothie, pack up my car, and start the drive back to Los Angeles. The beginning of my life intervention is complete. I have dropped about twelve pounds and feel about fifteen years younger. More than that, something sacred has happened to me that I will never fully be able to explain. I have entered some kind of powerful energetic field that has begun a true healing for me.

A clearing.

4

The Mighty DreamQuest

INT. CAR — DAY
LOUISE: We're not giving up, Thelma.
THELMA: Then let's not get caught.
LOUISE: What are you talkin' about?
THELMA: (indicating the Grand Canyon) Go.
LOUISE: Go?

—Thelma and Louise, 1991

Every Louise needs a Thelma. Every Ethel needs a Lucy. And vice versa. The most riveting tales usually feature at least one dynamic duo. I have cherished people in my life who are there for me through thick and thin, but in these weeks of "what's next?–ness," I need one person in particular: Nancy Hala, my longtime sister friend who is in the midst of her own middle-of-life reckoning.

Nancy (or Nance, as her near and dear call her) is gifted with a razor-sharp wit and an infectious laugh; her life force is palpable. We met almost three decades ago, through her now ex-husband, who was one of my creative partners at an ad agency in Chicago. Over the years, our friendship grew strong, even as our lives took different paths. I watched with joy as Nancy gave birth first to her son, Alex, then her daughter, Olivia; then, shortly after, and with the heaviest of hearts, she left her nine-year marriage.

While my job began evolving into an even bigger job, Nancy was juggling a thousand balls as a single working mom, building a thriving freelance-writing business. We caught up regularly during late-night phone calls after I got home from work and she had put her kids to bed. We shared all of our aches and pains into the wee hours. We consoled each other through the rough patches and donned our party hats when something needed celebrating. She always had a seat in my inner circle, and I had a seat in hers.

By now Alex and Olivia, who I'm crazy about, are fully grown and launched into big, bright lives of their own. And Nancy, a Fortune 500 brand strategist, is questioning her current position at a digital agency, the job that brought her to Los Angeles. It's become a not-what-she-signed-up-for disappointment, and to top it off, she, too, is still single.

As we sit in the backyard of Belle Vie, glasses of Chardonnay in hand, we continue our most trusted friendship deep-dive conversation about our individual reckonings and what we are going to do about them.

I share, "I feel like I'm right at the fork in the road. I have all these dreams I haven't touched, haven't made a priority, haven't even thought about in so long. Have I fucked up my entire life by putting so much on hold? And what if I'm only a bit past halfway through this life? What exactly am I doing with the next thirty, forty years?"

Nancy has mined some similar feelings.

"What I keep coming back to," she says, "is how I don't feel like I'm done yet. Just because I'm in my fifties and I've raised my kids, I don't feel like my life should be over. I want more, Sher. I want passionate love and adventure and great creative challenges. Why can't I have that, too?"

I listen intently. We've known for a while we are onto something that feels like a major shift, and now it's coming into focus. We feel better just talking about it. There is a fresh current in the air, a crackling electricity. All our talk is evolving into a new vision for our lives, a new vision for the middle of life. A conviction that it's never, ever, ever, ever too late to make the rest of your dreams come true. And if not now, when? Furthermore, if not now, maybe never. We are hearing our own message loud and clear.

Our conversations are ongoing as we sort out the details.

We wonder if we should partner and build a company of our own. We've talked about it in the past as a "maybe someday, wouldn't that be so fun" kind of thing. The idea of really doing it now is energizing. But can we be successful if our number one priority is self-care above normal business concerns? Yes, we want to be our own bosses, but most important, we want to live more joyful lives. Can we focus our company on that? Build a brand like that? A shared vision begins to take shape.

*   *   *

We agree to spend a solid year supporting each other in a personal commitment to radical self-care. We take it so seriously that Nancy and her cocker spaniel, Percy, move out of her condo in Marina del Rey at the beach and into one of my extra bedrooms in Los Feliz on the eastside of Los Angeles. It is a signal that our dedication to our declared middle-of-life reinvention is of utmost importance to both of us, as is our unwillingness to let a dastardly commute across the gridlock of L.A. derail our next steps.

We frame this adventure as our noblest undertaking, our Mighty DreamQuest (we are gals who love evocative language and a dramatic turn of phrase), and dub ourselves the founding members of our own dream tribe. (A tribe of two, but still.) Setting up shop at my dining room table, Nancy and I start to imagine what we want for ourselves. The areas of life that truly matter to us become our "pillars." They cover a wide range of human experiences like health, movement, food, spirituality, home, happiness, abundance, creativity, adventure, and relationships. What begins to take shape is a guidance system that we can use to help keep us on track. Day by day, we take our combined professional experience in writing, producing, and building brands then apply those talents in service to our new vision.

We discover we have a lot of dreams that converge, things that we can team up on. Being fit and healthy and more spiritually connected. Working on exciting creative projects of our choosing. Maximizing our capacity for happiness (not trying to make do with the lives we've created for ourselves thus far). We also have our own separate strategies to dial up the joy. The details look different, but the desired feeling is the same. Joy. And more joy. We long to experience more of the world through travel—Nancy to Paris, me to Tuscany and Rome. We want to partner with incredible men who are pursuing the lives of their dreams, too. We intend to expand our lives to include all of those things.

We have different stories, but both Nancy and I have fallen far short in practicing self-care. Taking care of yourself always sounds good until your to-do list starts to strangle you. Fits and starts and spurts and drops and dribbles—that's what executing it has looked like in my life. In a time crunch, in a sudden crisis, when anyone else needs something, self-care is the first thing to go. I remember clearly when best-selling author Cheryl Richardson shared the airplane metaphor on *Oprah* and left a whole planet of women gasping. She said you absolutely *have* to put the oxygen mask on yourself *first* (just like they instruct you to do if the plane is going down); then and only then can you help another. Otherwise, you are no good to anyone or yourself. It may have become something of a cliché by now, but I wonder if we've grasped its true import. For many women in the middle of life, understanding that intellectually is one thing; practicing it is another.

For those of us who feel the calling, this is the real opportunity. The middle of life is a moment for exquisite attention to self. That might sound like what we grew up believing to be "selfish"—an old-school red flag—but, in fact, it is quite the opposite. We are so busy trying to be of service outside of ourselves, volunteering until we drop, saying yes when we really want to say no, sacrificing ourselves until we are empty. There is no greater authentic service you can do for the world than to tend to your own garden—first. And then share the bounty.

And while you begin to care for yourself with steadfast devotion, you can't help but feel a new kind of love bubbling up, too.

My old friend, marketing genius and quasi-madman Gary Vaynerchuk, posted something on his Instagram feed that made me want to sprout wings and fly, it was so spot-on perfect. "Love yourself first. Love yourself *most*." Boom.

Dreaming up new dreams for each area of your life from a foundation where you love yourself *most*? C'mon. That's what was missing all along, right? For so many of us, we're either the one doing all the loving or the one waiting to be loved. Or the one waiting for enough time to love oneself. Or the one who's not really sure what it means to love oneself first, much less most. Or some combination of all of the above.

*   *   *

As Nancy and I take our longtime friendship to its next level, with our commitment to radical self-care front and center, there are powerful consequences. In the midst of our grown-up mind-body-spirit slumber party, our time together has become strikingly purposeful. It has become intentional.

Used to be, for years, we would meet for drinks or dinner, laundry-list all the stuff that had "happened" since last we spoke, seek validation for our complaints about anything or anybody who deserved some wrath, and decide that our venting had a beneficial effect. Then off we'd go until the next "stomp-around," as Nancy likes to call it. We loved to wisecrack, complain, and tell our victim stories. But the dark side of gossip, about others or about yourself, is that it starts to have a life of its own. You plant uneasiness in your gut, and when you finally diagnose it, you aren't sure anymore where it came from.

With intention, we decide to upgrade our time together and reduce our stomp-arounds to a couple minutes max. Then we dive right in to raising the roof with optimism and enthusiasm. Our conversations become more precise. We tape photos to my dining room walls and create huge vision boards of new dreams—something I never gave myself time to do before and would have passed off as a big waste of it.

Upliftment is a game of back and forth, and it requires that all parties suit up and play well. Once you commit to a better-feeling life experience, all the old negative ways of bonding with others stick out like crazy. You wonder why you would ever waste your time making yourself and others feel bad. You see that commiserating about unwelcome circumstances is a zero-sum situation. Nobody wins. Intentional friendship, on the other hand, amplifies everyone's victories.

When you say yes to making your friendships more about supporting each other in transformation, you are signaling to the Universe that you are willing and ready for more. It's no longer just inside your own head—it's been spoken to another human being and echoed back to you in their response.

Putting together your own quest begins right where you are. You may bump into some obstacles at the start. Maybe your kids are still at home, or your parents are dependent on you for care. Perhaps you are burdened by debt or feel entangled in relationships from which it's difficult to extricate yourself. Let the tenderness of your reckoning embrace all of these realities. Give yourself permission to expand your sense of possibility. The real question is, How can you do this *your* way? Is there someone in your life who may also be yearning for some sort of reinvention and who could be your anchor? Who else can be part of the tribe you gather for a weekly phone call, a daily check-in by text, a standing coffee date, or a walk around the neighborhood together?

In her book *A Tribe Called Bliss*, Lori Harder writes, "I am everything because of my tribe. When the shame from fear or failure tries to swallow me whole or tells me it's not worth it and to close off my heart again, they speak life into me. A tribe says 'me too, stay open or get up and try again' and suddenly you're not alone and the feelings loosen their death grip."

Nancy and I keep unfolding this new idea of the vast untapped potential for the role of friendship and tribe in our lives. In hours and hours of soul-level discussions we construct the framework that matters to us. Now. No more someday. No more one day.

Our overall commitment to the personalized recipes we create to live more joyfully stays pretty solid. But from time to time, we dip haphazardly into our old patterns; we go unconscious for a day here and a day there, or even more. The first thing to go is usually our twice a day TM (Transcendental Meditation) practice. Then we skip a workout or two or three. And then more bottles of Chardonnay get opened during the week than we had planned on drinking—for no good reason. But we catch ourselves, we regroup and gently redirect ourselves back to the lives we have decided we want instead of throwing our hands into the air and saying, "We're done. This is too hard."

No start. No finish. Just an ongoing becoming.

We are mostly cheering each other on when we aren't laughing hysterically at something or another. Nancy, a real cook, as opposed to me, invents all kinds of delicious vegan and vegetarian meals in my kitchen. She concocts dishes that resemble our yummy comfort food from our Chicago days— penne with "cheese sauce" made from carrots, cashews, and spices; "cream" of broccoli soup as good as anything you might sample at a midwestern supper club.

Our dreams are no longer stashed in an old dusty drawer in a rarely used desk; they are right on the table, out in the open, a priority. We begin and end most days with a meaningful discussion about the pillars of our new lives. Most important, we begin to get a sense of what life feels like when you make your own well-being top priority and you craft a personal recipe for achieving that well-being. Real. Good.

Our professional dreams are taking shape, too. We begin

working on a digital platform aimed at fellow seekers who feel like we do and also want to be inspired in their second acts. We have spent our lives as storytellers, each in our unique way, and now we are using the power of narrative to dramatically alter our own lives. Our mission statement reflects it: *The stories we tell ourselves are what make our dreams come true.*

We launch a podcast, *The Sheri + Nancy Show,* and begin having hilarious and achingly honest conversations about our victories and our stumbles, shared with a growing audience of listeners. We bring in well-known experts who add powerful inspiration and useful new insights to the mix. Every bit of content we create is about the helpful ideas we are uncovering as we begin rising up in our fifties to manifest new dreams. We discover that even the smallest practices that we adopt— like drinking enough filtered water or revamping our sleep habits—make a profound difference in how we feel about life overall. And talking about it regularly, both privately and on our show, keeps us enthusiastic.

* * *

At the heart of it, a dream quest is a spiritual quest. It can be a major awakening or a minor one, depending on where you stand and what you need. Its aim is to strengthen your connection to Source, to the Universe, to Nature, to your Soul, to Love, to Goodness—so that connection can become your

5

Chasing Beauty

Liposuction is not a weight-loss strategy.

—Plastic surgeon to me, 2000

I t began as all of my nutty schemes usually did—with an observation of something that worked fantastically for someone else. A colleague at *The Oprah Winfrey Show* had come
back from a lifesaving surgery looking like a million bucks.
When probed, she revealed that she had a little plastic surgery
and liposuction on her body to repair her "post-baby tummy."
We were all agog at what were obviously miraculous results.
And as a bonus, she seemed really happy. In the blink of an
eye I was in her surgeon's office quizzing him about the possibilities. Dr. Serious had a stellar reputation in the field. Our
meeting went something like this.

SHERI: "I am coming up on the five-week *Oprah* show winter hiatus, and I would like to schedule quite a bit of liposuction so I can get the fat sucked out, recover, and get back to work by early January."

DR. SERIOUS: "Uh, liposuction is not a weight-loss strategy. It works best for people who are at their goal weight and have an area that is out of proportion."

I didn't bristle at his observation. At the time, I needed to lose about thirty pounds. I was running regularly and avoiding carb-y bread-like things in a bit of a self-concocted Atkins-style eating plan. After seeing my colleague, I found myself so very hopeful that I had found a shortcut to the finish line.

SHERI: "Well, how much weight do you take out?"

DR. SERIOUS: "About eight to ten pounds." (That's what I heard anyway.)

SHERI: "Okaaayyyy. Can I ask that those pounds be removed from my thighs?"

DR. SERIOUS: "Well, yes. But I would do some from your hips, too."

SHERI: "Sounds like a plan!"

He was reluctant; I was gung ho—until I saw the price of this quick fix. I gasped, but then at lightning speed convinced myself that the slim new body that would be mine on the other side was worth eight grand. And may I say, as an aside, that none of my cohorts talked me out of it. In fact, my group of Harpo workout teammates seemed enthralled by what we all might discover from my pioneer-like bravery. Maybe this was the answer. Or at least a part of the mix.

On the big day, I got up early and did my normal thing, glanced at my watch and thought to myself "better get to the hospital" with the same tone I would use if I were heading out for a facial. The lipo was scheduled for the morning, and the surgeon's staff said I should be ready to head on home around 1:00 p.m. Friends were picking me up afterward, and maybe we'd stop for lunch if I felt up to it. Once at the hospital, Dr. Serious drew a bunch of lines on my body with a purple marker, someone gave me something to relax me, and then I dozed off . . .

And then I woke up. I felt foggy and weird as hell, like a Macy's parade balloon—puffy, huge, unbending. That was the fluid, the nurse informed me. They fill you to the brim with saline to suck out the fat. I was still drugged as I gently slipped on my overalls and rode down in the elevator in a wheelchair toward the car with a modest little bottle of pills and some instructions to ice myself a bit because there may be some discomfort.

The ride home (a grand total of 1.25 miles) took forty-five

minutes in minimal traffic. That's when I realized the actual meaning of the word *discomfort* is very subjective. I shrieked to slow the car down until we were crawling our way up Lake Shore Drive while people walking on the lakefront passed us by. Any pebble in the road would elicit a horrible groan from the core of my being.

And it got worse from there. A whole battalion of my near and dear had to stand watch and oversee my recovery for three days. My closest girlfriends propped me in the shower, stark naked, kept their shock and horror to themselves, and carefully, oh so gingerly, washed the bloody gore off of me. A beautiful scene this might have been had I done something super-important like giving birth, but this was tawdry in its pointless gruesomeness.

I took the pain pills, pushing the recommended limits, not understanding why I was running out of them so quickly. What were these anyway, just potent aspirin? In my mind this was a damn morphine situation. And if this wasn't, then what the hell was? The lipo holes—too many to count—spouted bloody geysers every time I moved. The sight of my own meat-like flesh was utterly revolting. I slept. Woke. And cried. Dosed myself mightily. Slept. Woke. And cried. And that went on for three full days. Lying immobilized in bed, I theorized that Dr. Serious and his lipo helpers used the word *discomfort* because not one of them had been foolish enough to undergo this madness. So they didn't really know.

Oprah and my workout teammates checked in, of course, and as I shared my experience in groans, I could feel that my pioneering had yielded real value for my workout buddies. Lipo would *not* be added to the mix of our group fitness plan.

Three months later, in the middle of a workout, I asked a friend, "Do you see a difference? Please tell me, do you see a difference?"

She answered, "Yeah, kind of, a little."

* * *

When in my life did this start? When did I begin this dysfunctional relationship with beauty? As early as the third grade, I think. I remember having an awareness that the tides had shifted. No longer were we all just a bunch of little bunnies bouncing off one another in the playground, unguarded, unfiltered, just exactly who we were. There was something new in the air, a pungent whiff of judgment. Which boys were cute. Which girls were cute. A new mix of analysis and labeling had shown up and had instantly begun sowing ugly seeds.

In my little grade-schooler mind, I quickly homed in on the label that seemed to wield the most power, the most desirable outcomes—"prettiest." And with each new school year, grade by grade, my conclusion was confirmed; I watched as those girls seemed to live better lives. They were skinny. They had boyfriends. They had cuter clothes. They were admired and envied. They were golden. The most shocking thing of all was the behavior of the grown-ups, who acted like they were under some sort of hypnotic spell. They treated the "prettiests" more like colleagues than children. The "prettiests" were usually further along on the physical development scale (read: bodies more like women), and I guess that made them seem older.

My "prettiest" theory followed me to high school. There I was a cheerleader (historically, a marker for some level of attractiveness) and was in the orbit of a fairly popular group. Yet inside I had judged myself cosmetically defective and all the Maybelline light blue eye shadow in the world couldn't make up for it. The night before prom I nearly burned my cheeks off with a cheap sunlamp to attain a "prettier" tan, then spent the entire dance dabbing the weeping blisters on my red moon-pie face. I should have been in the emergency room, not slow-dancing to "Color My World" with a wadded-up ball of Kleenex in my hand. Never satisfied with myself, in college I decided the Barbra Streisand *A Star Is Born* curly, short, permed "do" would dial up my glam factor, only to turn myself into a pumpkin-headed frizz ball.

The damage went far deeper than fried hair and a peeling

face. Somewhere in this decades-long "prettiest" toxic mess, I had come up with a shadow belief that beauty as defined by others was directly tied to being happy and, even worse, being lovable.

The "prettiest" scourge is a rarely discussed epidemic, but not long ago one of them outed herself. What she revealed about being considered beautiful has been downloaded twenty-five million times and counting.

In her acclaimed TED Talk "Looks Aren't Everything, Believe Me, I'm a Model," Cameron Russell acknowledges the free pass she has received as a "prettiest." She bravely concedes she won the genetic lottery and has benefited over and over again from what she calls "a deck stacked in my favor." Her refreshing honesty hit a colossal collective nerve. The perks of being beautiful are many. Finally, the truth from someone living inside that skin. But Cameron goes on to reveal that she and many of the women in her industry are plagued by horrible insecurity with all that focus on their physicality. She confesses what, of course, is true: it ain't always as great as it looks.

My inner self knows she's right. My grown-up-woman self knows she's right. But not all of me. It's fascinating to note that even now I hold some remnants of that flawed belief that being really pretty and really skinny is the key to being really happy. Why? Because I felt good in my skinny body many times. I felt more attractive, sexier, and more like a "prettiest." For a while. Until I would discover again that being a size eight didn't solve all of my problems. I was never able to stay in that "happier skinny" place for long because it wasn't rooted in real healing. I always forget that part.

That is the ongoing destructive cycle you experience when your original beauty story is seriously flawed. And chasing beauty is a sign you are walking through the world with a big crack in your self-esteem foundation.

There is, of course, an answer. There is a solution to the chasing-beauty melodrama. It's a big story rewrite: going back to your earliest memories of how you classified yourself in the looks department and how you internalized it. Yes, I said how *you* classified yourself. That is the real deal about how it goes down. Someone made a comment about your looks that stung a bit, a boy didn't return your affections and liked another girl, who you decided was better looking or skinnier or something more, and then off you went, leading yourself down a sinkhole of "not enough–ness." You gave yourself a severe evaluation way back when, and then all you could see was proof that you were right. Then, unwittingly, your behavior changed to support that story. You deflected any compliment or kind word about your looks like you were made of Teflon and anchored your beauty psyche to that rotten little story you made up about how you are not attractive. And you did that for years.

This solution will not be without effort. It requires keeping a careful watch on your reactive thinking and your judgments about your physicality and replacing the unkind stories with a whole new narrative. A narrative that you must construct with an entirely new language.

Have you ever had the experience of coming across an old photo of yourself from an era when you are certain you were fat, ugly, and completely unappealing in every physical way? Then you look at the photograph and you see that, in fact, you weren't any of those things. In fact, you would love to be that girl right now—inhabiting that body with that skin, with those eyes, with that smile, *now*. You would love to be *that* weight now! Or, you see the grade-school photo of you and your adult eyes can see so clearly that you were quite darling. Certainly not obese or unsightly. That is the evidence of the life-killing distortion with which you infected yourself. If you're not quite sure it's true, grab those old photos and take yourself back to that place and time. Remember how you felt about yourself? Remember how you felt about how you looked? Were you already starting to tell yourself that story of unworthiness? See if you can uncover the early threads of that disastrous narrative you were beginning to concoct. See for yourself how you were running that show, how you were making those judgments, and how you kept building on those themes with very little help from anyone else.

Again, the good news is there is a cure—and it's a spiritual cure. You must reframe your whole concept of beauty, redefine it with your own language, choosing each word carefully, and then put yourself smack-dab in the middle of that new story. You must be the very epicenter of what you believe is beautiful. And I am speaking about physical beauty here. You must practice your new view of beauty and include yourself as the focal point. Every bit of you. Never again can you entertain the dark exercise of taking yourself apart like the county coroner performing an autopsy—judging each piece of you separately and then adding up the tally. And you must make it routine to internalize compliments, letting them wash over you like a delicious summer rain, rather than dismissing the admirer who offered them as "just trying to be nice." It is imperative to your healing to give more airtime to those moments. You must tell yourself a brand-new story, infused with a new belief, a vow, to feed that story with words like *gorgeous*, *lovely*, *attractive*, *sexy*, *magnetic*, *glowing*, *adorable*, and, the best of all, *beautiful*.

It's a seismic shift, I assure you. It means that you also drop the pattern of scanning other people, judging them, and evaluating them. You must throw out the comparing mode that is just an old ruinous neural pathway from seventh grade that you never rerouted. When you cut off at the pass your tendency to judge and compare, suddenly everyone else's beauty is a reflection of yours.

I'm not against making changes or improvements to one's physical appearance. I think modern science is there to serve us—so enhance away. To each her own, I say.

Here is where purpose is everything. Taking care of yourself cosmetically, attending to your beauty and your body because it feels good to do it, has a different intentional grounding than believing you are more lovable and more worthy if you keep "fixing" yourself. So Botox your wrinkles, plump up your lips, microderm your skin, freeze your fat cells, or even get your extra pounds sucked out (surely they have made advances since I sampled that treatment). You will not be judged by me. Like most things in life, it's all about the "why." Do it to feel even more glorious, not to fill a hole or correct your own misperceived defectiveness. Do it because it's fun to dabble with lotions, potions, and maybe even a little procedure, because you know you already look good and it feels like fun to up your beauty game a snoot. Just don't do it to pursue a beauty that you will never find because it is inherently unfindable.

Because here's the truth: whether or not you are beautiful is not for anyone else to decide.

You must anoint yourself, once and for all, with your self-proclaimed beauty, or you will forever remain unanointed.

The Beautiful No

Beauty is in the eye of the beholder. It's one of the most famous lines ever written, and its meaning seems quite clear: we each decide what is beautiful because beauty is subjective. But I think there is a secret buried in those words. *You* are the beholder. You are the one who looks in the mirror. You are the one who tells the story. You decide.

6

Feel the Burn

Are you ready to do the workout?

—Jane Fonda, circa 1981

It's 6:00 a.m. and I'm on my hands and knees, lifting my right leg in a part–donkey kick, part–ballet arabesque for dozens of reps while wearing ankle weights on a bouncy wooden floor. The pounding rock track is playing at a deafening volume. Space heaters around the room heat the air to inferno-like temperatures, while huge fans blow the hot air directly into my face. My head is throbbing, and I'm trying very hard not to throw up.

I glance across the room to see how Nancy is faring. My vision is blurred, and I can barely make her out through what seems like a foggy haze, but she looks ghostly pale and seriously scared. Wait—she's on the floor—and not in a good way. My mouth starts to water. It's been less than twenty minutes, but I am barely clinging to consciousness, green around the gills and verging on a full-blown panic attack. I haul myself to my feet and stumble out the front door before I faint. I bend at the waist, heaving and gasping, as morning traffic whizzes by and I try to catch my breath.

It's day one of our new get-into-the-shape-of-our-lives strategy.

I am wondering if maybe I've put us in real physical danger. Nance and I have no business being here. I'm too fat, and we—the both of us—are not fit enough for this star-studded, cover-girl-model showcase. A scan around the room before I fled had revealed other women doing all the moves expertly, with the intensity of Olympic athletes and the elegance of Alvin Ailey dancers. You would recognize the famous ones from magazines and television shows, but since I once worked for a famous woman and understand how elusive privacy can be, I won't name them here. Suffice it to say that they are gazelle-like in their grace and thin limbed–ness, outfitted in the smallest Lycra workout gear, while Nancy and I have the presence of Lucy and Ethel on the candy-making assembly line. And though Nancy looks fine in her Lululemons, I am draped in a big black tunic-like *schmatta*, as per usual.

"This is just like me," I think, as my breathing slows a little and I slowly straighten up. Typical of how I like to run before I can walk, with well-intentioned enthusiasm as I put myself repeatedly in precarious positions. "Nice and easy does it" is not in my vocabulary when it comes to starting fitness regimes, as evidenced by the fact that I have taken this painful path many, many times.

Am I a unicorn? Or are there others like me who have invested small fortunes in equipment, outfits, and workout supervision only to bail after crossing the finish line? How much actual cash have I shelled out for untold annual gym memberships across the decades? Divided by the number of times I walked through the actual doors, I am sure my cost per workout is a frightful sum. I've Ashtanga yoga-ed right to my limits, spun myself clean over the handlebars and just missed cracking open my skull, and, for a brief shining moment, was a runner of real races. The training was arduous. Long runs on weekends (sometimes nine and ten milers), shorter three- to five-mile runs throughout the week. Two half marathons. I can't say I loved it. I can't even say I liked it. But it felt so good to be in my body, even if it required plunging myself in ice baths afterward. Those glory days always seemed so short-lived. Like I was a completely different person for ten minutes and then *poof*—back to the same old me.

I have felt the green-with-envy longing directed at those "lucky ones" who make moving their bodies as routine as brushing their teeth. I observe them like another species with whom I share no DNA. I marvel at how, just as they wouldn't dream of a day ending without at least two brushings and a flossing, so it is with their cardio, dance class, gym workout, run, hike, or speed walk. They just keep choosing moderate daily movement. Day by day. Year by year. Decade by decade. And they look and feel like the sum of those choices.

I've been a card-carrying member of another, less successful group—those who behave as if we can remake our bodies only through sheer force of will, along with the right pieces of stretchy gear and a sparkly new workout system with a complex program to master. In our little merry band, we are able to achieve success only by gritting our teeth and powering through until, alas, we let the air out of the balloon and fall back to our "who cares?" ways. Big bold start. Wimpy, out-of-gas finish. The results speak for themselves.

Now, I wonder, what is the cost of living out a story in which our bodies are huge obstacles to overcome?

In this middle-of-life moment, one thing is enormously clear to me: that was then and this is now. For most of my adulthood, on any given Monday after New Year's Day, going from zero to eighty-five miles per hour required only some gumption and Bengay for a few weeks to get through the initial body shock. Now, it's another ball game entirely. I am no longer young.

And yet, in the midst of my ninetieth do-over (averaging three per year for thirty years), I drag myself back into the oven-like room and resume the exercises, keeping my pleading eyes on the clock until it strikes 7:00 a.m. and the torture is over. Nancy and I gather our purses wordlessly and head outside to my car. We sit perfectly still as the AC blasts our beet-red faces.

Nancy is first to break the silence.

"What the hell was *that*? What *was* that? I can't do that again! Sheri???!!!"

I double over in a belly laugh, and so does she. We laugh and laugh until pretty soon we are weeping. Our first workout in the quest to once and for all create the bodies of our dreams has brought us to tears.

*   *   *

This insanity, as Nancy reminds me, was my idea. She had proposed we hire a personal trainer for the two of us—someone who would come to my house and work out with us in the backyard. But as is often my way, I wanted *more* than a trainer; I wanted a Khloé Kardashian physical transformation (say what you will, but she before-and-aftered herself in spectacular fashion). Here we were in Los Angeles with access to the fitness programs that created the best bodies in the world, and I wanted in. Why not shoot for the stars in our middle-of-life reinvention? One of the fun perks in my former career was meeting people in all areas of life who had accomplished amazing things and created huge businesses. One of them was a fitness mogul who had reconfigured some of the most famous women in Hollywood, and judging by them, the program was top tier.

I tracked the studio down, and in short order we were signed up for thousands of dollars of very difficult, private workouts. Turns out the "private" part is that you get your own instructor, but it all takes place in one room where everyone can see you. I noted this new information immediately as possibly detrimental to my success.

If our first day was a barn burner, things only heated up from there. We didn't always have the same instructors, as they liked to mix things up at the studio, but all were rock-star professional dancers of some sort. We went three times a week and could barely walk on our days off.

My biggest problem (and I had a lot of them) wasn't the jumping or planking or bouncy dancing or lifting my fat legs at impossible angles while my joints made sounds like popping corn. It was my projection. I saw snide glances and eye rolls at every turn. I even told Nancy I believed my most frequent instructor, a gorgeous, tiny, acrobat-like wunderkind, was irritated by me and my "need to take a break" pace. Nancy wholeheartedly disagreed, but I was unconvinced. That's the thing about merciless self-judgment: you start to believe everyone else is in on it, too. When I regained a portion of my sanity, I reminded myself of what I've always known: people are worried about themselves 98 percent of the time, and there is no room for a big dialogue in their brains about you. But it was easy to forget this bit of knowing while under duress.

We bravely continued to show up. Nancy gave up on the 6:00 a.m. time slot for something more civilized, and like the proverbial ships we'd wave weakly as we passed each other by. And then we hit our next round of hiccups. This workout protocol we'd signed up for involved a masochistic bait and switch. Just when we accomplished all the twisty-turny strenuous elements and finally managed to complete the required number of reps, everything was changed and we had to start over with a whole new regime. Devastating.

Equally devastating was watching myself march on in total compliance. Despite my résumé of "big-cheese boss–dom," I was willing to be pushed around by someone less than half my age and ordered to do things to my body that I was pretty sure could harm me irreparably. "What is this about?" I wondered. This weakness, this crack in my normal posture of "in-charge-ness" shocked me as I found myself balancing my entire weight on my left knee, while hanging by my right arm from an elastic band stretched from the ceiling as said knee joint sent searing pains up and down my body. I had a strong suspicion this was not what Jane Fonda meant by "feel the burn." But I did it anyway.

Let me just say, I came to adore those girls who trained us. But I seriously wonder, did they really know what they were getting into with me? Was there ever a discussion about my limitations, about how to avoid injuring me and how I was clearly in some kind of pain as I pressed on? I would guess that not many of those conversations took place, and they certainly never broached the topic with me. But I allowed it, it happened, and I didn't give up immediately. Nancy and I were getting results and losing weight. I continued to hobble my way through Mondays, Wednesdays, and Fridays like my dreams depended on it. And then it came to a startlingly swift end. Nancy's sore ankle required injections and rest, and my injured knee was now full-blown osteoarthritis confirmed by an MRI. The months that followed included steroid shots to quell the throbbing, searing pain and gel shots to cushion the joint; finally, I had to have my own platelets spun and injected to promote healing. My ortho doc gave me a new goal: avoiding knee replacement surgery for as long as possible. Nice.

Our Hollywood-style fitness fantasy was over. We had flown too close to the sun and gotten our wings seriously singed.

* * *

So what is the right fitness story for me now? I wonder. What is the vision? For as long as I can remember, it's been about getting skinny. It's been the elusive thin body I have conjured, achieved, loved, and lost many, many times. In fact, the skinnier I wanted to be, the fatter I got. Over and over again.

But this time, the plot is different. For those of us in the middle of life, we're in red zone territory now. This is no longer about wearing the daring, somewhat-bare dress to whatever occasion or hitting an important birthday at a lighter body weight so we don't go off the deep end. This is now about the very quality of the rest of our minutes *on earth*.

Here's what it looks like if you do nothing. At a certain point you can't touch your toes, put on a pair of socks, or lace up your tennies. Everything will have to slip on. Soon after that, getting up from a chair will require help from one of those Popeil pocket fisherman chair-raiser gadgets sold on late-night cable. Never mind the "elevator car" that you'll have to hook to your staircase. Am I exaggerating? I don't think so. I am way past the point where these concerns are idle. And I have been hobbling around on my throbbing knee as proof. This is the terrible truth that must be confronted and dealt with in the middle of life: if you don't find a way to make movement your friend and join that other group of day-in-and-day-outers, not only will you never have the body of your dreams, your reduced quality of life may make your life unlivable.

I begin a process of excavation to get to the root of my physical fitness starts and stops. Buried deep is a story of my own making that acted as an insurmountable barrier to success at any exercise. It goes something like: "This is hard . . . I hate this . . . I don't wanna . . . This is crazy . . . I don't care . . .

Maybe later . . . I'll start Monday . . . How skinny can I get if I do three workouts a day for a month?" Sentences, phrases, and sighs I've recited to myself for most of my adult life. In this situation, as with every other part of life, it comes down to the story I told myself. As is proven by my lack of results, my storytelling is powerful indeed.

But what if I rewrite it?

I start with words I like, words that move my spirit.

P o w e r.

S t r e n g t h.

R e s i l i e n c e.

F l e x i b i l i t y.

R e c o v e r y.

T r a n s c e n d e n c e.

F u n.

Hmmm . . . too soon for *fun*, but the other words land well on me.

Transcendence, in particular, is such a beautiful word. Now, in the middle of my life, I can see the unhelpful patterns I've lived over and over and over again with more clarity than ever before. My only way beyond them is transcendence.

I divest myself of the need for grandness, for the pageantry of the "big workout" that has been my Achilles' heel. I buy no new outfits. (Shopping is a telltale signal that I'm trying to create some fake motivation.) I already have enough equipment, so I work with what I have. No gym or program sign-ups (a sure indication that I'm about to quit in less than a month).

Instead, I review some sage advice from my friend and world-famous yogi Seane Corn, who shared her secret to starting a "practice" with Nancy and me on our podcast: "Don't make it all such a big deal. Keep your yoga mat by your bed and when you roll out in the morning, do fifteen minutes of sun salutations."

So I do. And I find the word *flexibility* comes to life for me. I now have that bucket-list consistent yoga practice I have said I wanted for millennia. It's not a super-lengthy complex practice, but it's mine. That's the beauty of yoga, Seane says, "It meets you where you're at." This is a new and delightful concept. I've always set ridiculously high fitness bars for myself in the hopes that they will propel me beyond where I'm at. Longing and suffering have been my companions in the midst of any of my total-body overhauls.

I take gentler steps. Four days a week, I do some strength training in my backyard. Nothing fancy or difficult. Bicep curls, deadlifts, squats, and so on—all exercises you can find for free on YouTube. Soon, I can feel a new layer of strength and power in my body. It feels good. I keep it simple. I resist the temptation to delude myself that I could become a fifty-something female powerlifter with plans to compete at nationals (as is my way).

On other days, I ride my Peloton bike carefully, do a no-impact run in the pool, or walk on flat ground. With each pedal stroke, kick, step, lift, plank, and downward-facing dog, my words come alive. *Flexibility. Power. Strength. Resilience. Recovery. Transcendence.*

My cohort in this middle-of-life reinvention is telling herself a new story, too. Nancy becomes a regular at Orangetheory Fitness, a branded workout that includes cardio and strength training in a group class. She can tailor it to her own level of mastery. I can feel the increased energy in her vibration when she walks in the door for one of our delightful business meetings. Her body is changing. Her mood is buoyant. She feels good. It shows.

We are healing. Sometimes we're limping a bit, but we keep moving. In our separate ways we both have come to the same conclusion: movement is one of the secret superpowers that enable you to extend your dreaming life. Movement is not just a means to an end, a penance to be paid for the perfect body. Movement is a privilege, a joy, even a kind of miracle. And our bodies are not obstacles to be overcome, or external objects to be whipped into shape. Our bodies are the vessels for our dreams.

7

OMG! I Forgot I Had Cancer!

I can't keep anybody alive forever, but I can help you
have a great journey. The yogis have a saying that when
you are healthy you can suck the nectar out of life.
That is healing at its most powerful.

—Dr. Rachel West, DO, to me, 2016

It's true. One of the biggest events in my medical history had somehow slipped my mind. Not long ago, I was in the midst of our podcast recording, unpacking various health and wellness modalities, when I suddenly heard myself blurt out: "OMG, I forgot I had cancer!"

Geez. Talk about letting things get away from you.

It was the year 2000, and I was toiling away happily at *The Oprah Winfrey Show* in the promo department. My coworker and darling friend Kathleen (aka MoneyPenny) noticed a mole on my leg. "OMG! That doesn't look good," she said worriedly, and urged me to get it checked at her new derm in downtown Chicago. Days later, the doctor took one glance at the black mole on my right thigh and screeched, "OMG! That doesn't look good!," setting aside what I imagined was her normal bedside manner. Flashbacks of sunlamps, thick tropical-smelling oil, and uncountable shivery spring break sunburns wafted through my mind. The jig was up. I would now have to pay the price. Perhaps the ultimate price.

Within days, the biopsy results were in and I was pronounced as having malignant melanoma, the deadliest form of skin cancer. I was soon carted off to surgery, where lots of tissue and lymph nodes were removed to make sure they "got it all" and to get a sense of whether it had spread or not. It didn't appear so. We would have to wait and see if it reared its head again. The world-famous melanoma doctor (whose nickname, I later learned, was "the Butcher") assured me that the crimson shark-bite-size scar would lighten with time.

I was stoic throughout much of the ordeal, or maybe numb is more accurate. But I do recall having a full-blown meltdown over the fact that my miniskirt-wearing days were now over—an item of clothing I didn't own and hadn't worn since the fourth grade. For a long while, I swathed myself in long sleeves, hats, and umbrellas, and made my poolside campsite in the shade. Gradually, my dance with the grim reaper faded from view. I moved on from the severest of prevention measures and eased on down the road to blissful forgetfulness.

*   *   *

Sixteen years later, I find myself in the midst of another health crisis, having completely erased any memory of the first one. This is equally serious. I have done my middle-of-life reckoning in my West Coast backyard and concluded that I am careening toward everything medically unwanted. I glean from the ethers that I am likely orbiting around various cancers, heart disease, maybe even a heart attack, inflammation on the verge of exploding, and goodness knows what else.

My self-neglect has stirred up some powerful fears. I have also diagnosed myself as utterly depleted, shockingly obese, and very sad. I know for certain I will not be able to dig myself out of my current state alone. I'll need a dramatic medical intervention. Caring, loving, attractive, crackerjack smart healers you might find in Shondaland. And where better to find them than in the city of the famous, who want to live forever and have the cash to make it so. Indeed, it turns out in my new town even something as mundane as an annual health checkup can be as glamorous as a walk down the red carpet.

I've been around enough rich and famous people to consider myself pretty well versed in how the world unfolds for them. As I've observed from my front-row seat, there are a boatload of drawbacks—ugly, soul-sapping things you wouldn't wish on anyone you loved. But there are a few aspects to being famous that are—hmmm—*awesome.*

My dad has a saying that makes my point perfectly. An evening out with him is all about securing "table number one." It's the table with the lake view or ocean view or most perfect position in the room; in short, the most enviable spot that will deliver the most wonderful stand-out evening. And this is what I've witnessed about being famous: basically, your life becomes an endless cookie jar of table number one experiences. In fact, your day-to-day becomes so table number one that in time you just think that's how things are. You scarcely notice the legions of humanity doing handstands for your tiniest desire. You become oblivious to the fact that rooms are discreetly temperature'd to your preference. That each little detail of every moment of every one of your experiences is precisely curated for your personal pleasure. Over time, for the famous ones, that good ol' table number one living becomes assumptive, and unless you fall from grace and lose your status, you never revisit regular life again.

In Los Angeles, even for the nonfamous, the opportunities for top-tier table number one thrills are a geographical perk. In 2015, when I moved here full-time from Chicago, my Angelino friends were eager to dazzle me with the possibilities of my new home base. Access to restaurants impossible to get into. The best seats at a concert. The car wash that comes to your house. But more than a primo stylist, a good blowout, or front-row seats, I needed medical help. Surely here, in the land of eternal-youth seekers, the secrets to health and wellness would abound.

In short order, I made my way to a fancy medical center where, for an enormous sum (a small portion to be paid by insurance), I would receive the best L.A. had to offer. I was interviewed, accepted, and scheduled, and in an eight-hour flurry I was treated to every single doctor's appointment I needed for a year, done in a single day. My feet were wings as I floated from office to office, kept company by my own special handler. Soon I was done with a general physical, pap, mam, CT scan, stress test, dental checkup, skin check, bloodwork, and all the rest of those lab tests. I was never kept waiting for more than a jiff. I drove home with a prescription for Lipitor in my purse (that I wasn't so keen on taking) and my head spinning about what I had just experienced. It was certainly table number one in some respects.

In the cold light of a few days' time, however, it was clear that while the fancy medical center offered a convenience factor for a busy gal like me, the experience was perhaps more about avoiding the hoi polloi in each waiting room and being made to feel like Beyoncé than about leading-edge preventative ideas. Style over substance.

I knew the leading-edge was out there. During my time at the *Oprah* show, I'd been exposed to the most current ideas in prevention. Stress reduction. Inflammation reduction. Nutrition enhancement. Sleep hygiene. The big decision for me, in the middle of life, was whether or not, once and for all, I was ready for substance. The kind of substance that requires a dedication to lifestyle measures that I had only previously toyed with.

One of the very best experts onstage and off is Dr. Mehmet Oz, "Dr. Practices What He Preaches," as I like to think of him. He is effervescent in personality and committed to learning what's next and new in health care and getting that information to the public as soon as possible. He is as well-versed in Eastern medicine as he is at the top of his field in the West.

My personal relationship with Dr. Oz was complicated, however.

Call it the "Dr. Oz is in the studio, Sheri, quick, run for a dark corner" kind of relationship. With his miraculous olfactory sensitivity, he could sniff out cigarette smoke and diet soda from a mile away (and I was still smoking and Big-Gulping). As a master healer, Dr. Oz could diagnose my issues in a nanosecond. Thus, I erected a kind of invisible boundary to avoid the confrontation that he would not spare me were he given the chance. This I knew: Oz has compassion by the truckload, but if you are a privileged, educated, adult executive producer who has access to knowledge, is aware of the facts, and continues to smoke, eat poorly, thrive on stress, and repeat behaviors that speed death, he is not excited about wasting his time. If I was willing to hear the truth about the state of my health, he would be willing to provide it; otherwise, we'd stick to a quick hello in the hallway.

It's embarrassing how long it took me to quit smoking. I was the last person still lighting up out of *anyone* I knew, even as my mom, aunt, and grandma battled lung cancer. Not until a new doctor I found in Chicago said, without a hint of judgment, "You'll quit when you are ready" did I get ready. She put me on Wellbutrin for a couple months to reduce the cravings and prescribed me the patch, and that was that. Now I get checked with CT scans every several years to catch anything that might crop up early. Sometimes, when I am stressed or on my third glass of Chardonnay, I miss it terribly. Then I remember how I felt being a smoker those last two or three years. I felt like an idiot.

What I did learn from Dr. Oz and the cool wellness pioneers he brought with him during our many show tapings was that in every culture on the planet there exist ancient recipes for health that would be state-of-the-art in our modern society. For example, Dan Buettner schooled me and our audience about the lifestyle habits of people in the Blue Zones, the world's longevity hot spots. In studying these diverse cultures around the world, from Greece to Italy to Costa Rica to California to Japan, what he found was that they had a surprising number of things in common that might explain why people there regularly lived to a hundred or more. And no, it wasn't about fancy medical clinics or expensive drugs. Instead, they followed simple lifestyle practices that stopped them from getting sick in the first place. Things like eating fresh, home-grown plant foods as the bulk of their diets, building movement into their lives, surrounding themselves with community, giving back, living with faith, and so on. Prevention being the name of their game.

Dr. Oz himself would come on the show, donning his green scrubs, and make the case for prevention to the American people and our viewers around the world by showing us the alternative—dried-up, rotten-looking organs yanked from dead bodies. He would often get rapped by naysayers for being too "neti pot woo-woo," but I knew he was deeply committed to science and his information was solid. Like all explorers who take us to thrilling new ground, he wasn't going to sit on the sidelines while layers of government oversight kept information out of regular people's hands. Our hands.

During the dozens upon dozens of Dr. Oz's appearances on the show, I listened and took copious notes. I had all of the information I needed to do a thorough reckoning about my health, but instead of taking a deep breath and making that commitment to myself, most of my good intentions went right to my "someday I'll get this together" list.

*   *   *

One of the major areas in which I ever so carefully guarded my unconsciousness was food. More specifically, animal foods. You see, as the granddaughter of a Swedish butcher and the daughter of a meat-cookin' mama, my love of meat was DNA deep. In my family, we never talked about eating meat as a choice because it was understood that a proper meal always included a hunk of it on your plate. Period. The end. Once Grandpa Art retired (and hung up his bloody aprons) and modern supermarkets popped up all over the suburbs, the meat we bought was wrapped in plastic on white Styrofoam and disconnected from any notion that it was once part of a living, breathing creature. And I liked it that way.

I always suspected, however, that my meat-loving ways were on shaky ground. I had never been a meat-on-the-bone kind of girl and preferred to stay as far away from clucking, oinking, and mooing as possible. The separation made it possible for me to love animals dearly and keep enjoying my sloppy joes and turkey burgers. Over the years on *Oprah*, I was exposed to all kinds of information about both the health hazards and the ethical issues with animal foods (remember the beef trial?). We went on vegan cleanses and learned about the horrors of factory farming and the devastating effects of those practices on our planet. I wasn't short on facts; I just chose to keep everything so compartmentalized that nothing could intersect and create any kind of new thinking. I wanted Bolognese, not enlightenment.

It was about a year before my middle-of-life reckoning that a chance encounter on my Facebook feed upended my culinary world. It was there that I first laid eyes on Esther the Wonder Pig: a six-hundred-fifty-pound beauty. Her two dads, Steve and Derek, adopted her in the belief she would be just a little micro pig, a house pet. Turned out they had been hoodwinked, but they kept her anyway, living with them in the house, and she soon became an Internet sensation. Transfixed, I watched video after video: Esther's grandma feeding her a snack in the kitchen. Esther opening the fridge door with her snout to get herself another little snack. And the pièce de résistance? Esther opening the screen door with her nose to have a "good girl" potty outside. These photos and videos were every bit as special as the photos and videos of my own beloved English bulldogs, Bella and Kissy, whom I would no more eat than a newborn baby. And with that realization my carefully constructed compartmentalization strategy came crashing down.

Esther was the morning bacon I had eaten for years. Esther was the Sunday ham I was raised on, Easter after Easter. Esther (who, by the way, loves to wear a variety of fashionable house-coats) literally rocked my shredded-pork-taco-loving world.

So that was it for me. I was done with pork, beef, chicken, turkey, and the rest of those kinds of meats. And soon even fish and seafood were off my menu most of the time. I'll admit that as someone who loves midwestern comfort food, it was a difficult emotional adjustment. Going plant-based can feel like a total uprooting of your social life and the deprivation of everything you have come to count on. Believe me, when you stop eating meat after having it two or three meals a day for most of your life, it ain't that great to go to a big backyard BBQ where the only vegetables are coleslaw and condiments. But without question it held some real health benefits. The sunlight that plants absorb agreed with every cell in my body, and that energy poured itself into my being in the best possible ways.

Now, a few years later, I have no doubt that this dietary shift is responsible for some of the positive changes I can see. And it gives me some much-needed confidence as I face the enormous changes that still need to be made. As I confront the many other areas of my life in which denial has been my default, I remind myself: I don't want to be the one hiding her cherished bad habits in a dark corner. I no longer want to be the person who hangs on kicking and screaming to behaviors that don't honor myself, my fellow world citizens, the most vulnerable of my fellow earthlings, or our one and only beautiful planet. I want to be a learner. I want to be open to new information. I want to be willing to know. I want to be willing to change once I do know. Mostly, I want to be willing.

* * *

Looking back on my life through compassionate eyes, I can begin to understand the patterns that brought me here. Just like a physician would take a medical history, I examine my own health background. What are my beliefs about wellness and where do they come from?

The story began before I did. There are lessons to be extracted from the "healthscape" of my parents and older relatives. I have seen early life-ending heart attacks, lots of cancers, and diabetes. Everyone was on reams of medications, having to devote half days each week to dispensing the prescriptions into those plastic pill holders. Most died fat or sad or very, very sick. Only the rarest few had a sweet, easy old-age passing.

Another thing I noticed, and it may be generational, was that my mom and the women of her time looked to doctors as if they were infallible pope-like gods. I also noted that, other than the occasional pediatrician, these doctors were all men. And even though those male doctor-gods were themselves tons of pounds overweight, exhaled their stinky cigarette breath all over you, and guzzled down booze as their sole stress-reducing practice, they weren't questioned on their wellness proficiency. That was perplexing to my young eagle eyes. If you're going to be the last word on health and wellness, you ought to be at least . . . *well.*

"The doctor said . . ." was the equivalent of Holy orders, especially when it came to medication and surgery (not so much when it came to cleaning up your bad habits). And I fell right in line. As I confronted the sorry state of my health, I could feel myself hoping to find the right doctor to entrust with all of it. Someone I could pass the physical buck to and not have to think about it anymore. The expert who would schedule me for all the tests I needed and give me my antidotes, be in charge of my apparatus, and tell me not to worry too much. I was looking for the authority on me. That's what led to my table number one day of top medical concierge-ness that ultimately left me feeling empty and alone.

It was time to face yet another middle-of-life truth. There would be no one single person stepping up to drive the Sheri medical bus. (Or any of the other Sheri buses, for that matter. The need-to-pay-the-mortgage bus. The income-taxes-must-get-done bus. The dishwasher-has-to-be-fixed bus. The A/V-stuff-isn't-working bus.) I realized I would always be in a semi-holding pattern until I faced the fact that I would be the one running my own show.

When actress-turned-wellness-advocate Kris Carr was

given a fatal diagnosis of an outrageously rare cancer in 2003, she realized she had to take charge fast. It was "Goodbye Broadway. Hello CEO of Save My Ass Technologies, Inc.!" she writes. She approached her illness as if "I was the CEO and the doctors worked for me. In order to survive, I needed to staff up posthaste." Kris decided to interview, select, and hire "her team" of professionals that would report directly to her, and then she would make all final decisions. Fifteen years later, Kris is in remission, living a gorgeous life of wonder, love, and green smoothies, and still firmly driving the bus of her health story.

In my middle-of-life moment, a big realization is creeping up on me. I need to do all of that, too, *before* I possibly get a fatal diagnosis. So that if that day ever comes, I won't be scrambling in a cortisol-spiking, life-shortening panic.

* * *

I begin. I reach out to healthy people for recommendations. Who is your doctor? Who do you trust? What do they believe? A popular body worker I like has an enthusiastic recommendation, so I book an appointment with her naturopath in Santa Monica. Dr. Rachel West is a trained physician who is more likely to recommend meditation and yoga than pharmaceuticals. That is the path I have decided to walk. I want wellness medicine, not sickness medicine. She and I agree to do rigorous testing, above and beyond anything a purely conventional approach would do—even the table number one kind. Blood, urine, saliva, poop, breath—it all goes through the testing wringer. The results come back, and we review them like we are reviewing a Fortune 500 P&L. I want to know: the good, the bad, and the ugly.

There is a lot in my body that is working very well. I have already made many changes in my habits and choices, and the reports say that I am reaping the rewards of those decisions. Still, there are very serious things I need to address to make my health dream real.

My cholesterol vastly exceeds even conventional standards, which aren't really as rigorous as they should be, say some experts. Even though my intake of animal products is minimal, I have some genetic issues there (my dad's cholesterol was once over 500, and he has been on medicine for decades). My markers for inflammation are high. I have heavy metal toxicity—mainly lead and mercury. My vitamin D levels are way too low. Vitamin B12—low. My adrenals are wiped out from years of fight-or-flight stress. And while I am making great progress with losing weight, continuing to increase movement and refine my diet will be key to the results I seek.

I take in Dr. West's suggestions for next steps and make

my own decisions about what will be best for me. I sit with it. I noodle on it. What makes sense? What aligns with my own intuition?

I decide to do a detox program for heavy metals. I take some supplements and mix up Medical Medium Anthony William's plant-filled recipes for heavy metal detox shakes. I think he's really onto something, that Anthony.

Lots and lots of leafy green vegetables become an even bigger part of my protocol. I believe in my bones we are on the verge of universally acknowledging the power of plants as our personal preventative medicine cabinet. The information about these health benefits is growing exponentially. I've already experienced the power of making plants the center of my diet. I want to optimize that diet even further and see the correlation not only in my medical chart but in how I feel each day.

I also give myself a serious talking-to. In this age of discovery about food and nutrition there is bound to be dissent. That is how progress is made. Pronouncement. Skepticism. Progress. Three steps forward. One step back. But *two steps forward net*. That's the headline.

I know I'll be confronted with conflicting information. "Cauliflower is good for you!" "Cauliflower is poison." "Eat more beans." "Beans will kill you." "Yay for nuts." "Nuts? Just say no!" In our modern Internet age, the good news is that we're all empowered to access the very latest in health and nutrition research with the click of a mouse. The bad news is, the Internet loves a good hook, and too often that means highlighting anything shocking or controversial. So it takes some work to read beyond the headlines, find trusted sources, and look for congruency rather than contradiction. When you dig a little deeper, you find plenty of common sense advice that experts agree on, and you learn to discern the nutritious information from the junk. I vow to do that work, and, above all, not to use the mishmash as a sly excuse to throw in the towel and head straight for a drive-through.

Time passes. I feel better. I almost feel good. My new habits are paying off. My blood tests are improving. It's working.

I am now far enough along in tending to my health that I can see the person I used to be with the honesty I aspire to and the tenderness I now require. I see that for so long I had a deeply worn groove. Unhealthy, risky patterns I shared with millions in my human family. White-knuckling it, hoping we won't get sick. Resisting thoughts about the state of our bodies as if by not thinking about it we can ward off disease. Telling ourselves that we really are powerless and that a so-called "balance" of healthy and unhealthy will keep us safe. Hoping our less-healthy habits don't do us in. Wanting to believe that we are the lucky few who can smoke and drink and eat hunks of artery-clogging fat and live past one hundred, though our inner selves know it's not likely. Quickly forgetting the scary moments that threaten our fragile denial.

I am not a perfect patient on my path of wellness. I note that being older adds some new challenges. I find, for me, it is much easier to gain weight than it used to be, and it was already fairly easy. I'm talking about ten-pounds-in-three-days kind of weight gain. And there is a new tendency I am experiencing toward a menopausal Santa-like belly that needs extra attention or takes on a life of its own. Some joints can ache after exercise, which makes increasing the difficulty of my workouts less appealing. When stressed about anything, I still feel an inclination to numb it with cheese and throw a make-myself-feel-better party that turns into why-did-I-do-that-feel-bad regret.

But I keep taking next steps, and I keep my body dreams crisply in focus. My positive new story about feeling healthy is continually getting revised, reviewed, and repeated to ground myself in what I really want. I am beginning to like the feeling of being in charge of myself. I am growing more and more fond of the ever-evolving woman I am becoming—the woman who would never choose to dwell on the fact that she survived cancer but certainly wouldn't forget it ever happened.

I am also noticing the difference between the two voices in my head that are sharing the duties of driving my aforementioned medical bus. There is the old voice that wonders anxiously, "When will this be done so I can go back to my old ways?," and the newer voice that asks lovingly each morning, "In how many new ways can I rise?"

One of those voices will determine my fate. One will grow stronger, and one will grow fainter.

As the CEO of me, it's my choice who gets to drive.

8

I Did Everything Wrong
(and It Turned Out All Right)

*When I graduated from this hallowed institution,
I wanted a leather briefcase with important
papers in it (didn't matter what they were), a
suitable position in a corporate structure, and a
generous vacation policy. And once I put on that
practical suit of "I have to earn a living" clothes
you couldn't pry them off me for a long time.*

—My commencement address, the University of Iowa, 2013

I remember an ominous feeling building inside me as my graduation from college approached. What was I going to become? It was more and more clear that I wasn't going to have that sorted out by the time I tossed my cap in the air. And while I celebrated hitting the finish line heartily, I was feeling a sense of dread about becoming self-supporting for the first time in my life.

It can be a haunting question. What do we want to be when we grow up? The decisions can loom large and feel so very permanent. Like we are signing up for something forever and there will be no unsubscribing. We just don't have perspective yet on how our lives are going to work. We don't realize that it is unlikely to be a straight shot to blissful fulfillment for anyone.

There are some rare people (the tiniest of populations) for whom these big-life moves appear to be an easy-breezy slam dunk. They seem born with an absolute knowing about what they want to do and what they were meant to contribute to the world. For instance, my cousin Molly knew she wanted to be a teacher from the time she could stand in her little baby toddler shoes in front of a blackboard with chalk in her hand. And now she's a fourth-grade teacher. No detours. No meandering. No messiness.

Then there is another group. They may not be certain what the specifics are regarding the work that will bring them grat-ification, but they have a reasonable plan. They might begin in a corporate training program or start working on a graduate degree. Their professional futures aren't plotted out on a map, but they are heading in a direction that feels pretty good.

Then there are the ones who don't have a clue and feel anxious because everyone else seems much further along. Those are my people. Growing up, I was temporarily enthralled by a series of occupations. I wanted to be a paleontologist. Author of the history of Poland. A popstar. A marine biologist. And finally, a physician. But by the time college graduation rolled around, my ambitions had narrowed and grown vague. Here's what I did know: it would be good to have a business card with a respectable title and an entry-level paycheck. Any further details were fuzzy.

Today, when asked, "What do you wish you could tell your younger self?," I say this: "Worry less. You're going to do a lot of things wrong, and it's going to turn out all right. But spare yourself some pain, tune in to your inner compass at the start, and make sure it's pointing you to where you want to go. Your dream is happiness, not just a spot on an org chart. Your dream is joy, not just fattening up your résumé."

I believe we all have an inner compass, a directive that lives quietly behind the scenes and really is the mastermind behind most of our life decisions. This compass is a kind of patterned inclination—do we generally lean in the direction of the good stuff, or do we give our compass some attention and rechart our course only when we've made a mess of things?

When engaged proactively, our inner compass can help steer us toward good-feeling opportunities that create positive outcomes. "Where do you want to go?" you say to yourself. "Toward more happiness," you decide. It sounds obvious, but without that deliberate conscious choice, we set ourselves up for a bumpier journey that takes us a long way around to where we really want to go.

That's my story.

*   *   *

Heading into college, I felt pretty confident, having been near the top of my class of very smart Catholic girls at Carmel High School. And I knew exactly what I wanted to study: medicine. I had set my sights on a white lab coat and my very own stethoscope, and I had decided "Dr. Salata" had a melodious ring to it. My dad, Stan, tried to be a voice of reason.

"Sheri, you are so squeamish, we have to cut your chicken off the bone," he half pleaded, before wisely suggesting, "Why don't you just take some classes and see what you like? No need to rush into anything."

But I knew better. Doctoring was important work, and I most definitely aspired to end up doing something important. I had watched enough *Marcus Welby, M.D.* and *Medical Center* with the very dreamy Chad Everett to know this profession had all the trappings I was seeking. The next question was, what school would I attend to begin my medical training? Dad, a Northwestern grad, sold me on the noble traditions of the Big Ten. Then, thanks to a brochure in the mail filled with bucolic photographs of a charming small town with a river running through it and a heralded med school, the University of Iowa in Iowa City was the standout.

I loved the town, I loved my ADPi sorority sisters, I loved my fellow students, all twenty-five thousand of them. I loved tailgating and the genuine esprit de corps on game-day Saturdays; I loved every single thing about my new college life except . . . the pre-med classes. These subjects required a real rigor that I was not prepared to put forth. And the torture began at 8:00 a.m. every day with math for biological sciences, followed by a frightfully science-y chemistry class.

By the end of the semester, in a stunning turn of events, I, a lifelong mostly-straight-A honor student, was on academic probation. It wasn't just the early hours or even the incomprehensible subject matter. No, it seemed I had taken a crazy shine to my new social life unfettered by parental oversight. I was eighteen years old (the legal drinking age at the time), and there were a good solid eight to ten bars and clubs that were filled to capacity every night of the week. My life had quickly become a disco inferno.

While my extended family prayed novenas for my comeback, I surveyed the campus, strategized my options, and rapidly transferred from pre-med to the business school and a marketing major—mostly because that was what my roommate was studying, and it looked doable while maintaining an active social life.

"Sensible," said Dad, trying to disguise his relief. "That's using your head, Sheri." Business was something he understood and, more important, he believed this path would allow me to put a roof over my own head someday. That was key.

Upon graduation, I had no big plans, so I drummed one up: a cross-country move to Dallas, so I could feel like I was "making things happen." I had elected not to participate in on-campus interviews (I was too busy on my farewell party tour) and instead planned to wing it once I landed on Texas soil. That turned out to be a serious miscalculation since everyone else had done the important pre-planning and secured entry-level positions; I was way too late to the party. I ended up at a regular old employment agency in desperate straits. My cash was just about running out—I was sharing a studio apartment with a generous high school friend (thank you, Janice) and at a certain point I was going to have to pay my share. So I took what was offered and reported for duty as a typist in the legal department of a real estate title company downtown.

We midwesterners are heart-of-America kind of folks, raised to show up for work with what I call "lunch pail dedication," which means you stay at your desk through lunch and give your life's blood to anyone who gives you the opportunity to serve for a paycheck. And dedicated I was. Even at these early stages, a theme was emerging: I would take a position meant to be a temporary stopgap and attempt to turn it into my path to retirement. And my succeed-under-any-circumstances approach appeared to reap real rewards.

Soon I was promoted to second secretary to the general counsel. It was a Melanie Griffith *Working Girl* kind of moment. From anonymity in the typing pool to a more important typing job on the executive floor. I was on my way. Sort of. It was clear that in order to become the person for whom someone typed instead of the person spending her life covered in white type-erase powder and typewriter-ribbon ink, I would need to go back to school and become . . . a lawyer.

In my spare time, I studied hard, soared on the law school entrance exams, and set up a call to give Mom and Dad the exciting news. I made my pitch, and they listened quietly. On matters involving big cash, Mom would defer to Dad, so I knew who needed to buy in. In the Salata family, my dad, Stan, occupies the spot as the patriarchal wise one, the guy who will negotiate your car deal to get you the lowest price, the magician who can fool anyone with his sneaky card tricks and April Fool's Day stunts: in short, a strategic mastermind.

"Sheri, we *love* the idea of you going to law school. Good

for you, honey, for studying so hard and taking the test and doing so well. We are so proud," he smooth-talked me, long distance from Chicago.

My antenna was up. This was a little too easy.

"We think it is great that you finally found your path." He slathered it on some more. Then he lowered the boom, "Of course, you will have to work during the day to pay your rent and go to law school at night, but we will support this decision one hundred percent."

With that one phone call home, my legal-eagle ambitions were dashed. My father knew me better than I knew myself (and often reminded me of that fact). He sensed that my newfound passion for the courtroom had more to do with my desire not to have to continue to report for duty each day at the old salt mine and less to do with a genuine love for the law. He was right.

I was miserable. I was not great at the duties of an actual secretary, and my boss often seemed on the verge of an emotional breakdown. It was time to move on—and not a moment too soon—before I had a breakdown of my own.

From there I entered the scrappy world of retail sales at a high-end toy store. I couldn't hazard a guess as to why, except someone offered me the position, and since I was about to melt down at the title company, I took it. I was the assistant manager (meaning I worked the night shift). I was fascinated to discover there is a whole world of toydom with as many professional opportunities as there are stars in the sky. I began to plot my entire future work life through the lens of toys. Maybe someday I'd even run a toy company. The holidays rolled around and semis backed up to our mall dock on a regular basis, requiring linebacker-like heaving and unpacking and pricing and stocking the precious cargo of thousands of sugar-plum-fairy dreams.

But this year was a year like no other, because 'twas the fabled release of the Cabbage Patch dolls. Holiday tensions mounted as supplies ran low, inciting bloody mall battles between desperate moms who were all coming apart at their fa-la-la seams. I was literally bashed in the head with a purse by one of those crazed women after I uttered the despicable words "Sorry, but we're sold out."

When that high-end store went out of business due to a limited demand for toys that cost the same as a new car, did I have a heart-to-heart with myself about what I had learned from the experience and what kind of work I might really enjoy? Did I make an adjustment? Try a new path? No! I had no time for self-reflection, I had a career to build. I moved on to another mall in Dallas—and another toy-store chain. This time I was really in charge, signaled by my massive ring of manager keys—clear confirmation I was moving up in the world. But this was more of a discount operation. The toys were kind of junky, and the mall was sort of seedy. The best part of the whole thing was my boss, Rodger. He was a tough-talking, hard-nosed, chain-smoking badass who could scare the wits out of anyone but had somehow taken a shine to me.

Rodger could sense I wasn't loving my day-in-and-day-out, but he kept me going with his sharp wit and unflinching support as with each passing moment my job began to feel like meaningless toil. When he abruptly left the company, life at the cheap toy store lost what little shimmer it had. I continued to sniff and sneeze my way through mountains of stuffed animals made God knows where, but it began to be hard to get out of bed. A depression rolled in that I struggled to good-mood my way out of.

My internal compass was really showing itself. An unhelpful pattern was emerging that informed my budding life as a professional. When I got so miserable I couldn't stand it, it was time to move on, but not a moment before. For years, my inclination to make the best of a bad situation ruled my day to day. I ignored the twitches—the weird feeling that "that's enough of that"—and gutted it out until I could feel a total psychological meltdown knocking on my door. Feeling awful was my only trigger to make a change. I had unwittingly made misery my compass. It turned my twenties into a bit of a shit show. I would sit in a pot like a lobster not acknowledging my skin was turning red until I was pretty much cooked alive.

One thing I did know by the end of my toy-store era: retail was *not* my calling. Buuut . . . since I had already invested a few years in it and had some actual real jobs on my résumé, I kept going. No stopping and regrouping for me! And the biggest retailer in the Southwest was 7-Eleven. In the eighties in Dallas, Texas, Southland and its gazillions of 7-Eleven stores on every corner was a big, big deal, as evidenced by their gleaming corporate towers that epitomized the height of success. Corporate towers that I intended to make my way to, tout suite.

Unfortunately, before I would be brandishing a briefcase and wearing heels and a suit, I would have to do my "smock-wearing" time in the stores. I would train to be a certified 7-Eleven store manager. I would become an expert at all the tasks you can imagine that go hand in hand with such a position. In my mind, I played down this part of my training, telling myself that it would be but a blink of an eye.

What followed was the toughest eight months of my life. A convenience store "boot camp" that in my imagination was only too similar to the real thing.

On a corner in a suburb of Dallas, I ran a three-person operation. From 7:00 a.m. until 3:00 p.m., I would work the cash register, make coffee, count the cash, order all the merchandise, clean the shelves, sweep the floors, fix the Slurpee machine, and deal with a thousand people who looked down their noses at my station in life. If my 3:00 p.m. to 11:00 p.m. clerk showed up, which was not always the case, I would go to the back room, finish my deposit, do some more cleaning, and head to the bank on my way home. There I would pray that the phone wouldn't ring with the dreaded call that the night clerk (11:00 p.m. to 7:00 a.m.) hadn't shown up. On those awful nights, I would get dressed, drive back to the store again, work through the night and the next day until someone relieved me. Oh, and did I mention that my store was open seven days a week, twenty-four hours a day, 365 days a year? This brutal, bustling retail ecosystem provided the perfect excuse to continue to avoid the deeper questions: Was I happy? Did I like the direction my choices were leading me in? Was I energized by this work?

I stayed at 7-Eleven for about three years. I got certified, ran my own store, and then became a supervisor, which meant I had a group of stores reporting to me: six times the fun. I dressed as a clown to gather change at intersections for Jerry's Kids in 110-degree heat, delivered a baby boy in a parking lot, and worked as hard as I had ever worked. My store managers were an amazing bunch. I am a third-generation American, and this was my first exposure to modern-day immigrants. One was the son of a South Vietnamese diplomat; another was related to a Saudi prince. All of my managers worked hard for their bit of the American promise as they joined me in working toward a better life. Their hope was humbling. For the rest of my days I will never enter a convenience store without a sense of reverence for the tough assignment of running a shift while being judged as "less than" by a good number of the customers.

As the much-prayed-for day approached, the day when I would leave the stores behind and head on over to a tidier, grander life at corporate headquarters, I had a chilling vision: me, at sixty-five years old, sitting behind my 7-Eleven HQ desk, having spent my life there doing some kind of something. My heart beat wildly as I struggled for breath in a full-blown panic attack. Suddenly, I knew in my bones that I was at the wrong company, doing the wrong job, living in the wrong city.

My life was entirely wrong.

"Sheri, you are doing fantastic—you are next in line to be promoted to the big time," said Don, my smiley and supportive boss, when he called me into his office the next morning.

"I need a Kleenex," I gasped, as I broke into sobs then tried to pull myself together. "I have to quit."

"Whaattt??? You are on track for a big promotion."

"I miss my family in Chicago," I fibbed a little.

"You can move in with me and my family," he said.

"Ahh . . ." (Wow, this was going to be harder than I thought.)

I felt bad. But the truth felt too harsh to say out loud: "If I stay here, I will wither and die. My soul is literally suffocating. I'm so unhappy I want to drown myself in a vat of liquid nacho cheese whiz, which, by the way, has become my daily diet." Those were the words I could not say to this lovely man, who had promoted me, touted my talents to the higher-ups at corporate, and always had a moment to listen when I needed support.

After six years in Dallas, and a rather weird assortment of jobs, I had failed in my quest to get my business card filled out with a snappy title. I had failed to identify a very clear and exciting career path to importance. My Texas experiment was a total flop, and it was time to skulk home with my tail between my legs, cloaked in my own unhappiness.

Gone was the salary. The 401k. The health insurance. The stability. Not to mention any slight sign that I was making something of myself.

I arrived on my parents' doorstep in Lake Villa, Illinois, with my brother, John, who had flown down to help me drive back, along with everything I could pack into my little Renault Alliance and my dog, Addie Lou. It was the middle of the night, since we had decided on a whim to drive straight through. Understandably, Mom and Dad were disheveled, having been woken up with a start, but they also looked scared, and I felt sick to my stomach. Reflected in their eyes I could see the big fat mess I'd become.

That year I turned twenty-seven. Since I am not to the

manor born, that is not the end of my career story. We'll get to the good parts later, but it does bear taking a look at this compass business. I'd like to tell you that I took stock, recognized my own patterns, and cleaned them up as I camped out at Mom and Dad's, but, in truth, it would be years before I could see what had been driving me for so much of my early life.

My particular inclination was not to move in the direction of what felt good, what made me happy, what vibrated joy; it was simply to move away from awfulness. When things got to feeling really hopeless, dark, and empty, then and only then would I check in with my inner compass and realize it was time to make a change. Imagine the suffering you could be capable of causing yourself with that manner of walking through the world. You literally set yourself up so that misery is *always* the endgame, always waiting for you around the bend.

*   *   *

In 1985, just a few years before my humiliating Dallas departure, writer Joseph Campbell sat down with legendary television personality Bill Moyers for a historic interview. The transcripts yielded some of the most profound, beautiful thinking of our time. Campbell said:

> *If you follow your bliss, you put yourself on a kind of track that has been there all the while, waiting for you, and the life*

that you ought to be living is the one you are living. Wherever
you are—if you are following your bliss, you are enjoying
that refreshment, that life within you, all the time.

Oh my goodness, he's talking about ease and flow and
alignment and all the good stuff the Divine would love to heap
upon us and our magnificent lives. That's how it's supposed
to be.

His simple but soul-stirring words probably floated right
over my budding spiritual newbie self back in the eighties.
I recall when it became popular to say "Follow your bliss,"
but I couldn't relate much. "She does exactly what she wants
to do" was not a compliment when I was growing up. It was
the description of a willful, self-indulgent person who would
no doubt be the object of lots of disapproval. Something I
hoped to avoid back then.

But J.C., in his own way, had gotten to the heart of what
ultimately, decades later, has become my compass theory. He
and I are in full agreement. When you begin by believing that
the Universe is on your side and conspiring on your behalf,
and then you recognize that feeling good is a sign that you
are moving in the direction of your heart and soul's desires,
you have signed up for a far easier road. When you commune
with people who are fellow uplifters, that feels good. When
you create your own atmosphere of appreciation and wonder,

that feels good. When you do what you love with people you love, that feels really good. And when you feel really good, good things happen again and again and again.

When happiness is your compass, misery becomes impossible.

It's always the simplest of things, isn't it?

9

The Beautiful No

I'm sorry, you're not what we're looking for.

—Someone from *The Oprah Winfrey Show* on
my answering machine circa 1993

I t was a terrible blow. And tears were shed. Even so, I wasn't totally shocked. I knew I was out of my lane when I applied for a job as a promo producer at *The Oprah Winfrey Show*. I was an ad agency producer at the time, and typically the two worlds (advertising and television) were very different. In the ad world, a team of creatives (spearheaded by a producer like me) would spend months on a thirty-second television commercial or "spot" for a brand, product, or service. At *The Oprah Winfrey Show*, a promo producer would create a thirty-second commercial or promo for each episode, and it would be written and produced overnight.

Still, the rejection was depressing. After so many career fits and starts, the prospect of working on *Oprah* felt like *Eureka! I found it! The place where I belong!* I had imagined it so powerfully that I was sure it would happen. But the voice on my answering machine said otherwise, and the answer was no. I would not land that dream job. As far as I was concerned, that no had a finality to it. There are many people I admire who never give up on things, who keep going back for what they want—over and over and over—and hope they get to yes. People who never quit trying. Ever.

I was not one of them.

With some nagging worthiness issues, some shame-avoidance policies, and a secret fear that I was not what anyone was looking for, my appetite for further humiliation was nil. The dream was dead, and I was going to have to pull myself together to drum up some freelance producing work to pay my bills. In my spare time, I could tend to my bruised and disappointed feelings as I wondered, at thirty-three years old, what on earth I was supposed to be doing. Was I going to have to start over, yet again? I was beginning to feel old and tired.

* * *

Six years earlier, I had moved back to the Midwest from Dallas, Texas, after my various jobs as a typist and toy-store manager and my stint at 7-Eleven. I was simmering in a stew of self-pity in the basement of my mom and dad's house, wondering if I would ever find my way. I had lost faith in the Universe. I had no trust that all would be well. And every time our eyes met, I could read my mom's crushing fear that I was all washed up at twenty-seven and might possibly never move out.

Enter my angel, Perry, the dashing fiancé of my best friend from high school.

He knew I had moved back from Texas and very considerately called my mom and dad's house to check on me. When I shared my tale of unemployment and no prospects, he took pity.

"Why don't you get out of the suburbs, drive down to the city, and I'll take you to lunch?"

My mind raced. I hadn't left the house in weeks. My nine to five consisted of lying around watching soap operas and game shows, wearing wrinkly pj's, a ponytail, and glasses, and feeling sorry for myself. Having to rally some cheery for a public excursion was daunting, but I knew in my heart it would make me feel better if I finally washed my hair and got out of the house. I jumped in the shower and primped myself up.

After an hour's drive, I arrived at Avanzare, a swanky white-tablecloth restaurant in downtown Chicago where the city's notables hobnobbed. Perry and I had met a few times over the years when I was back in town visiting from Texas. I knew about his interesting life in the advertising world as a producer of television commercials. He was now the executive producer of an agency—maybe he'd have some good advice for me.

I took note of his über-cool presence: faded jeans, velvet slippers, collarless white shirt, navy jacket. He looked like Ralph Lauren's twin brother sitting there sipping on champagne and smoking a Dunhill Menthol. He reeked of creativity and excitement and elegance. We ordered salads and wine, and he spoke to me thoughtfully and kindly about how I had ended up in my current state. There were moments during our conversation when I had to control the underlying catch in my voice. I just wanted to put my head down on the table and weep. It was such a relief to be seen through his eyes as someone with great potential. Maybe my move back to the Midwest could be the beginning of really good things for me. As our two-hour lunch wore on, he infused me with hope. I could build a great life in Chicago, he said. I could start a whole new career. We talked for a long, long time as he bolstered my shaky confidence. And then . . .

"What do you want to do?" he asked innocently.

"I want to do what you do," I heard myself say.

That was the moment. The change-your-life-forever moment. In a movie you'd see the world literally flip over on its axis—the tides would reverse in slow-motion; the heavens would part—as an entire destiny was instantly rerouted.

My answer had come out of nowhere. I hadn't a clue I was

going to say that. But something had sprung forth from my soul, and suddenly what I most wanted in the world was crystal clear.

He exhaled long and slow.

Then he told me he'd see what he could do but made no promises. I found out later that he had gone back to his office and spent the next several weeks moving people around to make a spot for me as his secretary. The pay was just enough to live on, sixteen grand. But I would have done it for free. It was an honest-to-goodness big break.

I was posted at a desk right outside his door, my IBM Selectric softly buzzing throughout the day. Over time, he trained me step-by-step in how to produce television commercials . . . and only slightly let on that my secretarial skills were not exactly as advertised. He allowed me to go with him to television shoots and edit sessions, recording and music sessions—all the creative and technical aspects of making those commercials you watch at home. When he deemed I was ready, I produced my first radio commercials and then later television spots. He took me on my first trip to Hollywood, where I nearly passed out from joy when I finally laid eyes on the famed Hollywood sign up in those gorgeous hills. We stayed at the rock-star hideaway—the Sunset Marquis Hotel—where Paul Stanley of Kiss was cavorting in the pool about ten feet from me. We dined at Spago, a chic restaurant where Wolfgang Puck had made a name for himself. I was in my creative element, and for a long time I was challenged and happy. I produced an array of commercials for a wide variety of clients: banks, shampoo, hair spray, amusement parks.

For six years I stayed at the agency, which was located on the top floors of Chicago's famed Merchandise Mart. Across the river, the number one television show in daytime was making national news on a regular basis. I rarely watched, since I worked full-time, but there was something very special about Oprah and *The Oprah Winfrey Show*. It wasn't often that a daytime television show impacted millions of viewers so strongly on topics across the board—everything from marriage to motherhood to managing finances to interviews with the biggest stars on the planet. Soon newsmakers made their way to the west side of Chicago to give the exclusive interviews that were coveted by every network on the planet. The Oprah phenomenon was a real force.

I loved the creativity and artistry of my producer role, but more and more I wasn't as enthusiastic about the content I was producing. I wanted to work on something I really cared about. I wanted my work to have a major positive impact on people's lives. I wanted meaning—and that's what I believed was happening at Oprah's production company, Harpo Studios.

With Perry's blessing and in a pique of optimism, I sent my résumé and a video cassette of my television commercials to the head of the department who did the daily thirty-second spots for *Oprah*. I could feel the drumbeat of destiny pulsing through my veins. For weeks after sending off the package, I had that weird relationship with the phone, like when you're afraid to leave the house because you'll miss your new crush's call. Well, they did call, and despite devoting untold hours to "phone monitoring," I was out. The message on my answering machine held the grim news: "Thank you for applying. I'm sorry, you are not what we are looking for."

And with that, my worst fears were confirmed: I was not *Oprah* material. I went on with my life, charting my course as usual by that compass called misery.

Soon after, I left my job to freelance produce at other agencies and see what other kind of creative work was out there. My discovery? Freelancing—or more precisely, drumming up work—was a daily grind of dialing for dollars and leaving messages for people who rarely called back. Selling myself for a premium price was not my strong suit, and it soon showed in my bank account. My inner circle rallied round with moral support—and a casserole or two, dropped off by my ride-or-die pal Nancy when business was really light.

Before long, my day-in-and-day-out once again consisted of lying on the couch watching soaps and seriously wondering if dreams ever came true.

Then, a light at the end of the tunnel.

My beloved friend Erin came through with an interview at J. Walter Thompson, a big-time hoop-dee-doop agency where she worked in the upper echelons and had some pull. The job was perfect for me—a senior producer position on big brands. I pulled myself together and got ready to sparkle.

The interview couldn't have gone better. Mr. Executive Producer Man popped my VHS into the player and watched five minutes of the best thirty-second commercials I'd produced. He seemed enthralled.

"Sheri, I know we have a place for you. You are just what I am looking for, a great fit, the salary is lots, and the company benefits are too many to list," he confirmed. "I'll be in touch with next steps."

The champagne, cocktails, and Grand Marnier neat with Diet Coke back (my nightcap of choice) flowed at our regular Friday-night watering hole, where my friends and I celebrated mightily. "Let's not get ahead of ourselves," we kept saying, before toasting my new job-to-be. I felt a flood of relief. In my elation, I crafted a story that accounted for all the false starts, sudden shifts, and ups and downs I had endured. They were all leading to this golden moment. And damn it, once I was working on elite national brands, I would make the "meaning" happen. There was nothing to do but go home and wait for the formal offer and my start date.

Monday. Tuesday. Wednesday. Thursday. Friday. And then it was week two. Nothing. My phone messages went unanswered, a knot began to form in my stomach, and the following Friday, a J. Walter Thompson envelope arrived.

Dear Ms. Salata,
At this time we have nothing available.

Sincerely,
Mr. Executive Producer Man

Later that night, the regular happy-hour crew and I gathered again. I was teary-eyed as they tried to comfort me. To be so close to an outcome that seemed so fated, so right, to have my expectations so buoyed and then so curtly dashed felt bad. We analyzed that chain of events backward and forward and concluded that none of it made any sense. Not one bit. An unsolvable mystery. (Later, we learned Mr. Executive Producer Man just decided not to add to his team.)

Hours passed, and one by one my loving friends peeled off and went home. As last call loomed, I teetered on the barstool, and Erin and I—both in our cups—waxed philosophical.

"What is it that you want to do? Forget everything that's happened, what is it you really, truly, truly want?" she quizzed me.

"This is going to sound crazy, but I really think I'm supposed to be at *The Oprah Winfrey Show*," I said, shocked to hear myself say it. It had been a long time since that rejection.

"Well, try again. Or mail yourself in a box and pop out with your résumé or something creative that will get Oprah's attention."

"I think that's the kind of thing you see in the movies. In real life it's just desperate and stupid and will make me look crazy. Oh well. See you at happy hour next Friday."

* * *

I shuffled through the next week, padding around my little condo in Old Town, a neighborhood in Chicago, my spirits trampled. I had no more moves. At some point I threw on some sweats to run out for food, and when I got back, I saw I had messages. I ignored the blinking light. Whoever it was would have to wait until I felt like talking again.

The next afternoon I hit Play.

"Hi, this is so-and-so from *The Oprah Winfrey Show*. We were cleaning out an old closet and found your VHS and résumé. Are you still available to come in for an interview about some freelance work?"

And that is how it happened.

A new department head, Harriet Seitler, had been hired at the show. Harriet had made her mark at MTV, done phenomenal creative work, and wanted promo producers with more advertising agency experience. She had her staff dig through stacks of old applications, found my dusty VHS tape, and liked what she saw. I did one week of freelance work for her and then she hired me for her team.

I was thirty-five years old, fourteen years out of college, and had started over from scratch more times than seems rationally possible when my career dream came true. And all because of that beautiful no.

Had I gotten the fancy senior producer position, making big cash with great benefits, there is not one chance in the world I would have quit that job weeks later to freelance at *The Oprah Winfrey Show*. Certainly not when they had already rejected me soundly once before. Not one chance.

I would have let that once-in-a-lifetime Harpo Studios opportunity walk on by with regret, but after so much uncertainty I would have stayed put and convinced myself that I needed a sure thing more than I needed a chance at a big dream.

The *only* reason I was available for *Oprah* was because I had received that life-altering, stunningly beautiful no.

I didn't have the perspective to see the splendor in that no until years later, when I suddenly had a flash of insight: none of my experiences in television, none of my glorious *Oprah Winfrey Show* moments, would have happened if Mr. Executive Producer Man had hired me.

Then I wondered: Was it bigger than this one instance? Had I stumbled upon a spiritual revelation? Is it possible that *every* no in my life has been a beautiful no?

How about this one? The recruiter who turned me down in the fall of '81 for a General Mills grocery-store sales-rep position in Houston, Texas. I can't even remember what he looked like, but I love that guy, wherever he is. His feedback after my interview: "She doesn't really want this job. This isn't the right fit for her." Thank you, good sir! What a gift!

Then there are the one or two men who didn't love me back. I had fantasized about marrying these men, bearing their children, and building a little trilevel paradise with them. At the time, on some unconscious level, they knew better than me that we were ill matched and on very different life tracks. They would have become ex-husbands, no doubt, with all of the inevitable complications. Thank you, beloveds. *Mwah! Mwah!*

The list goes on.

Listen, this may be a bold statement, but if we could collapse time and recognize the beauty in a no right when it arrives, no matter how disappointed we might feel, I think we would have mastered something fundamentally important about living happily ever after. I can't imagine the emotional riches that would accompany the demonstration of such spiritual savvy.

I play a game with the lives of people I love. People I know really well. I scan through their big disappointments, those I witnessed personally or those I just know in intricate detail from years of shared storytelling. I look to unearth their beautiful nos. And I gather my proof that pretty much every single one is a big gorgeous gift.

So far, I can't find a no that isn't.

10

The Greatest Show on Earth

THIS . . . IS . . . YOUR . . . LUCKY . . . DAY!!!

—Oprah Winfrey, *Oprah's Favorite Things,* pick a year

Strolling down Carpenter Street on the west side of Chicago that bright August morning in 1995 and stepping through those fabled double doors for the first time was like entering the Emerald City. The atmosphere was kind of magical, with a feeling that life-changing business was afoot. The free coffee bar was always stocked to abundance. That's where I'd begin my day. The supervising producers, producers, assistant producers, and production assistants scurried back and forth from the actual television studio to their offices like their hair was on fire. On taping days, we'd produce one show in the morning and another in the afternoon. The studio audiences would electrify the entire city block as they joyfully waited for Oprah's arrival on set. I would watch at my desk and take notes then dash off to write and produce a thirty-second spot that would usually air the next day. It was a do-or-die adrenaline rush that felt like being *alive*, and I had never experienced anything like it before.

Each week we taped up to six shows. Some were just wildly entertaining, good old-fashioned fun, and others stirred my soul in the deepest way and sent me home mulling the meaning of life. I had finally given focused attention to my inner compass, and each day I headed in the direction of happiness. I was thirty-five years old and starting over *again* in an entry-level position, but I had never felt better about my life.

The show was entering its tenth season when I came on board in 1995. It was a powerhouse television hit—number one every single day, with monster ratings. Living legend Paul Simon had written and performed a new theme song to mark the occasion. "Ten years come and gone so fast / I might as well be dreamin' / Sunny days have burned a path / Across another season . . ."

In the Harpo hierarchy, there was no question that being a promo producer, my new job, was much lower on the ladder or, as I characterized it, "in the basement." The show producers ruled this fairy-tale land, and indeed, as I would come to see, this was as it should be. What they were putting out into the world every day was special, and nothing else like it was on television. All of us in support positions, like we promo producers, got to give our blood, too, but only after a show had been produced.

In those early days, I received the best advice from my former boss about how to view my career inside this new world. He said, "Listen to me carefully. I have seen what you can do. Don't ever worry about getting promoted. Keep your head down, do the job right in front of you, and I believe Oprah will pluck you out." I took his advice.

I began my journey in the promo department and stayed there for seven years. Next, I was moved over to the show to become Oprah's Book Club producer, then was promoted to a supervising producer, and in August 2005, after another ten years had come and gone, I got a message to report to Oprah's office.

"I'd like you to be the executive producer of the show," she declared.

It was a stunning statement.

"Why?" I stammered.

"Because you know my heart."

Weeks later, I began my five-year stint as the executive producer of *The Oprah Winfrey Show*, a post I held until the final credits rolled.

*   *   *

We often don't know we are in the midst of some truly glorious days until we grow older and more reflective, and then we gnash our teeth but good. Why didn't we know how great we had it? Why didn't we savor those experiences? Why didn't we realize we were in the best part of our lives? But I was lucky this time. I knew from day one at *The Oprah Winfrey Show* how this experience would be the most profound of my life. I'd had enough jobs that were less than glorious to know the magnificent ride this promised. I knew that my employment at Harpo Studios was more a mission than a job. I knew that I would be a part of history, not an annual report. I knew it the day I started working there and each of the thousands of days that followed. Not that there weren't tough times or dark moments, but when I would work through the million little crises or even the ordinary irritations and aggravations and see it from a bird's-eye view, I had no doubt I was in the midst of something so extraordinary that its like would never come again. Talk about your glory days.

And none were more glorious than those days leading up to the very last *Oprah Winfrey Show* ever.

*   *   *

Tuesday, May 17, 2011—The United Center, Chicago, Illinois

"Are you ready?" asked our long-time director, Joe Terry.

Ready? I wasn't sure, but it was too late now to be anything but. I was sitting right behind Joe in the control room trailer in the executive producer chair, at Chicago's United Center. The supervising producers and producers, having finished their last-minute checks, were scrambling inside for the start of the show. I adjusted my headset, which would be my only form of communication with our assistant director and, ultimately, with Oprah, throughout our marathon taping. The monitors in front of me showed a sea of fans, already on their feet and amped up for the start of the biggest production we had ever attempted.

Attempt being the operative word here. This production was so big that one of the most legendary live-event producers in show business had cautioned us that what we were trying to do verged on the impossible. Most shows of this scale and featuring this much star power were methodically pre-produced over ten to twelve months, with full-time attention from a dedicated team of producers. We, on the other hand, were dreaming this up with weeks to spare while maintaining our normal taping schedule. Even the availability of our location had been shaky for weeks as we crossed our fingers during the NBA and NHL playoffs. The Chicago Bulls and the Chicago Blackhawks needed to clear out so we could move in. On time.

You could say we had bet the farm on this extravaganza. For starters, we had booked every guest and produced every solitary moment of two blockbuster hours of television without Oprah knowing a diddly or a doo. Even up to the last minute, she wouldn't know where she was being driven for this taping of two of the final episodes. Our only instructions to her were: doll yourself up and wear comfortable shoes! This kind of thing was decidedly not her cup of tea; she was usually hands-on with all of the shows, approving every guest and reviewing every script. But she agreed, after a loooooonnnng think, for the "good sport–ness" of allowing her world-class team of producers one last chance to do their thing.

Yes, we were on the edge of the tree limb, and I could hear it creaking. But there was one thing we all shared in our company: the belief that we could do anything. And we certainly believed we could do anything if it was for Oprah.

For the past two days, those beliefs had been tested around the clock as we loaded in enough equipment and rigging to do a U2 concert, a Super Bowl halftime show, and the Oscars—all at once. Now we faced the final test. We were excited and nervous and steely in our resolve. The energy backstage was equal to the thunderous energy building inside one of the biggest basketball stadiums in America, now our studio.

It was go time. Joe and I conferred. There was not a minute for a final rehearsal, no way to check tape, audio, or anything technical—something we had done without fail for every other show. For the first time I could remember, we were going to wing it.

The producers and I held hands for a moment for good luck.

"Ready, Joe," I replied.

"Here we go," he answered.

Five. Four. Three. Two. One.

Down went the houselights and big booming music flooded the arena for the thousands upon thousands who had jam-packed the stadium for this special taping.

The announcer (or "Voice of God," as it's respectfully called in show biz) came over the deafening speaker system while the audience went crazy with anticipation.

"Ladies and gentlemen, making her four-thousand-five-hundred-fifty-ninth appearance on *The Oprah Winfrey Show*, please welcome . . . Oprah."

Out walked Oprah Winfrey to a standing ovation that went on forever. She stood there laughing and smiling and looking around like "what's happening?" because she had no clue what was coming next. The biggest stars on the planet had snuck into Chicago and stayed out of sight. Now, they were hiding out in special lounges we had created backstage, waiting to pay tribute, entertain, and say a heartfelt thank-you to the woman who had supported them and their work for twenty-five years. We gave it a few more beats, and then one of my favorite guests ever, Tom Hanks, acknowledged his cue, took a deep breath, and strolled out to surprise Oprah.

We were off to the races.

* * *

Sitting in the control room for that United Center taping, I felt nostalgic, sure. I also felt the import of the moment. Right before our eyes a cherished part of modern life—a part of life we could all count on for an hour a day, Monday through Friday—was morphing into a historic legacy.

For twenty-five years, *The Oprah Winfrey Show* had been a touchstone in American culture. To this day, I meet people who say they were literally raised by Oprah through the television screen. And others who say they never missed a single show. Not a one.

What Oprah Winfrey, her brilliant founding executive producer Debbie DiMaio, and their band of young genius producers had created two and a half decades before was a virtual lightning rod. Millions of women from every walk of life were instantly drawn to *Oprah*. Women who needed to be seen, to be heard, and to feel a sense of belonging. To talk out in the open about the things that mattered to them.

As the seasons ticked on, one after another, the show continued to hold the top slot even as other popular talk shows hit the scene. But no one else was Oprah. And her office shelves filled up with Emmys to prove it.

New producers came on board. Superstars emerged within the ranks. And the shows grew wider and deeper in texture and resonance as Oprah and the team grew right along with the audience.

A book club was launched. An angel network was born. A "wildest dreams" season took to the road with Tina Turner. New bars were set. And those hurdles were cleared with room to spare.

By the time that last season rolled around, *The Oprah Winfrey Show* was basically a prime-time special that hit the air in the daytime five days a week. The shows were multilayered, with live guests, gorgeous taped stories that framed a concept, and a show theme that evolved out of a specific intention (something Oprah required). The ante had been upped twenty-four times with each new season, and now those of us still at Harpo Studios would be charged with delivering the final one. Season 25. The one that would usher the most successful daytime show ever into the record books.

I had been with the company for fifteen years by then. It was my fifth year as executive producer, and don't you know I was feeling the pressure of that final season. A bundle of nerves all summer, I wondered what else could we possibly do to top ourselves? The audience expectations would be soaring based on years of rip-roaring wild-ass creativity. It meant we would have to rise up like never before to land this legacy. Fortunately, this team, this crew, and the entire staff had proven time and time again that meeting the moment was what they did best.

In August, we came back to work following summer break and prepared for our annual show-ideas pitch meeting with Oprah. Our lives had been ruled by each new season's launch, but now we knew that was all about to change. There would never be another gathering like this with the team working together, getting ready to produce a whole season. And second, for the first time there were reality-show cameras shooting us behind the scenes for a docu series to be aired on OWN, Oprah's cable network that was launching in five months. Few savvy producers who know the reality-show game would delight in being put under such a microscope. It added to the pressure.

The meetings with Oprah were a success. The producers pitched their hearts out. And by the end of our long days of brainstorming we had our season-premiere-worthy show idea. We high-fived and went to work.

Once back at the studio, we fired up the dream-making machine, and Season 25 was underway. That first audience was fall-to-the-floor out of their minds when a jumbo jet rolled out into the studio and Oprah shouted those stunning words, "We're . . . going . . . to . . . Australia!" We had launched our farewell season exactly as we'd hoped.

As each week passed, we taped show after show and walked through a myriad of last times. Last season premiere. Last appearance of this or that movie star. We revisited classic Oprah topics that had stirred controversy and made headlines decades before. One by one, we were slowly ticking off the last 140 *Oprah Winfrey Show*s there would ever be.

Our rock-star graphics department created a special calendar so we could count down the season with our staff. Oprah would rip off a sheet after a show taping and sign it with appreciation to the show producer who had delivered once again.

Just as they had for years, our studio audiences continued to show up, day in and day out. Grateful to get tickets, they would line up outside the studio dressed to the nines because they were going to Oprah's "house." And she returned that reverence. Our top-drawer audience department was an extension of Oprah, and they knew she wanted her audience to be treated like guests in her home.

The last season felt different for me than the ones that had come before. There was a sense of more ease, more flow than usual. Our show calendars filled up to the brim as notables wanted one more chance to sit across from Oprah. Publicists and managers swarmed our booking department to be included. And we saved some of the best for our two-part "Oprah's Surprise Spectacular" at the United Center.

And what a night it was—we had never done anything on that scale. The most entertaining part was watching Oprah's reaction as each segment of the show revealed the next surprise guest, the next jaw-dropping performance, the next ugly-cry-into-your-hankie tribute. All those well-deserved thank-yous served up like a fantastical Broadway show. It was like Christmas morning watching Oprah unwrap that love and gratitude.

The whole thing was blessed with "Amazing Grace," as sung unforgettably by Ms. Aretha on that memorable night. When confetti filled the arena, it was done. And it had been flawless. Not a graphic miscued. Not a walk-on ill-timed. Not a musical note missed. Our director Joe Terry and his crew had been perfect. Tara Denise, our lighting and production designer, had turned that arena into a producer's playground, and the result was a wonder to behold. A three-dimensional tree made of lights "grew" from the floor of the arena to the highest of heights as the audience gasped and clutched at their hearts. Our team had delivered so far above and beyond that you could hardly conceive of what they had accomplished—the magical ideas, the incalculable scheduling, the millions of details that made those hours on stage sing and made Oprah weep to high heaven. Every single person in our company had contributed their heart and soul and blood and sweat and tears. They left everything they had right there in that arena on that Tuesday night, May 17, 2011.

Then, there was only one show left, the final show. And the producing honors belonged to Oprah. With barely a moment's rest, still reeling from that oh-so-glorious night at the United Center, we spent the weekend before the final taping in lockdown in my office, Oprah and I. She talked; I typed. And when we were finished we had the last show's script, filled with her lessons, her treasures to share with a worldwide audience whom she called her greatest of loves. "All sweet, no bitter" was how she characterized the end of this era. Paul Simon had done a beautiful updated rendition of the "ten years" show theme.

"Twenty-five years have come and gone and that story's still unfolding . . ."

I think of the poignancy of his lilting voice and Oprah turning to the studio audience and the cameras one last time and waving, then making her exit before the credits rolled.

The Oprah Winfrey Show was television history.

Our history.

My history.

11

My Epic Fail at Work-Life Balance

How do you achieve work-life balance?

—An audience member at every speech I've ever given

I knew the question was inevitable. At every panel, speech, or any other kind of appearance I got asked to do, the first question from the audience was always a lock:

"What is Oprah really like?"

"Just like on TV," I'd reply.

Next up was usually "What were your favorite shows?" Many. What were my favorite moments? Thousands. Easy. Easy. Easy. Then, invariably, came the question that was much harder for me to answer. Because it just felt bad. Like skulk-away-in-shame, hang-my-head bad.

"How do you achieve work-life balance?"

Once the dreaded question was uttered, I would do a little

automatic mini—life review right there in my head. When you work from 7:00 a.m. to 9:00 p.m. most Mondays through Fridays, plus untold hours on the weekends, all while being on call 24/7, it's difficult to claim anything resembling "work-life balance." I worked a lot, and when I wasn't physically at work, I was thinking about work. My "children" were English bulldogs, and most of my social plans had to be made at the eleventh hour. I could feel my own tongue tsk-tsking.

Usually, I'd deflect with humor. I'd gulp. Smile conspiratorially. Wait for the chuckles. Then I'd jabber on with some mumblings and ramblings that I can't recall anymore. What I do remember is the feeling of failure and squirmy self-consciousness that tore through me each time I had to answer that question. I'd stand there feeling tried by a jury of me and found guilty of being unbalanced and therefore wrong.

Then, unexpectedly, like a bolt of lightning through the crown of my head, I had a breakthrough. I was onstage being interviewed by Debbie Phillips, founder of Women on Fire, at their annual conference. When she went to Q&A, it took only a couple minutes for that question to come up. I took a big breath, unclenched my innards, and connected to a truth buried deep within me. When I spoke it aloud, not only did I shock the jam-packed audience, I shocked myself.

"I don't believe in it. I don't believe in work-life balance," I said.

From my perch I could see the whole front row of these "women on fire" instantly light up with hope.

In the moment, I released my discomfort and grasped a new way of seeing this issue. Why did I feel bad about not achieving something that I didn't even believe in? First of all, I didn't set out to achieve balance, I set out to make some big dreams come true. Moreover, the whole construct of this so-called work-life balance seems to revolve around failure. The very nature of balance is about being out of it and coming back into it. Rinse and repeat. Now you've set yourself up for a wobbly game of maneuvering back and forth on an imaginary Twister mat to make your life "right." "Am I in balance?" "Am I not?" "Am I now?" "How about *this*?" "Is *this* any better?"

In those years of go, go, go, my career was a fantastic way to spend the lion's share of my time. I had wanted to fully inhabit the high-flying, dynamic creativity; the globe-hopping excitement; the profound sense of meaning and service that came with my job. I was fulfilled by my accomplishments, and that was what I wanted. That's not to say I couldn't have taken better care of my health and made my love life a priority. I could have, but to my everlasting regret, I chose not to.

And as for that make-believe lifestyle called work-life balance, what is it anyway? I think it is supposed to mean that each area of your life receives perfectly parceled-out equal attention. Ask any working mother about the success of that strategy. Or someone working three jobs to pay the rent and trying to keep herself healthy and sane. Or someone running an international conglomerate, overseeing thousands of employees. In any given moment, do they consistently meet that fanciful "balanced" criteria? Of course not. It's a bit of a language thing I'm pointing to, but as you write the story of your life, words most decidedly matter. And when you have set yourself up for failure repeatedly with a construct that doesn't fit your choices or your dreams in any capacity, life just seems hard. For me, *balance* is a word that works in architecture, design, or geometry; it finds usefulness in yoga tree pose but not so much in regular old bill-paying human life.

In any given moment of our lives, we are deciding what matters most to us. We direct our attention and energy to whatever that is. It's a dance of flow, not a pie chart or a mathematical equation. There are times when what we do to pay our bills and contribute to the world is our chosen priority. Sometimes that's not what our happiness formula calls for. I've come to see that the formula can be continually tweaked by paying attention to it. Making little adjustments. An ebb and flow run by choice and guided by what feels good, not by guilt and shame. Take out the self-castigation and you can run all the areas of your life as you see fit.

If the phrase *work-life balance* doesn't send you into a swirl of guilt and not-enough-hours-in-a-day-ness, then balance away. You probably define the term differently and aren't judging yourself mercilessly. But if it makes you think you have to put a drop ceiling on your professional dreams because you can't have what you want in life; if it makes you feel as if you are failing in every direction you turn, then consider letting it go. Stop saying those words. Stop using that phrase. Give it a proper burial and unburden your heart.

But how do you spend your free time? It was generally the follow-up to the balance question.

Once I understood my truth about that "work-life balance" business, the issue of "free time" became crystal clear. I'm not in the gulag, trapped against my will, where I have absolutely no choices. *All* my time is free time—determined by my choices. Choices I am *free* to change at any time. Even when I spent very long hours on staff jobs, all of that time was my free time, too. If I ever chose to whine or moan about my work "have-tos" I was just plain wrong. Even back in the day when my budget was squeezed within an inch of its life and I was sweating out a $19.95 a month credit card payment to Montgomery Ward, I was still free to choose how to spend my time (no matter what kind of victim-based stance I took). My life unfolded directly from my choosing this way or that way. I was then, am now, and always will be free.

Saying goodbye to that thinking has settled something inside me. It has quieted down that voice of mine that says

"You're not doing enough here, there, or everywhere" or the story I made up about a million "But I have tos" that sometimes made life feel like a prison. Deconstructing my belief system about job and work and life was turning into an awakening where the more I freed myself from my old thinking, the more free I felt.

If there is no "work-life balance" agenda and all my time is "free time," then what does that mean for the mighty divide known as work life-personal life? I pondered that concept and gave it a vision. I pictured a gigantic barrier where on one side you are running a brand, managing a store, leading a team of many to a company goal, running your tax business, leading the local Boy Scout troop, running the express lane register at your local Safeway, or performing any number of noble career pursuits, and on the other side you are scrapbooking, doing laundry, framing photos of your children, and planning the next family picnic. Living two different lives. Two separate lives. In some cases feeling like two different people.

That's how I lived for a long time. There was work. And there was everything else. But now that feels like a *Leave It to Beaver* episode—being trapped in a time when men wearing hats and carrying briefcases came home after a long day at the office to a pipe and slippers.

Maybe there is a different way to see it. Maybe we can have one life.

One life.

Integrated.

Connected.

Whole.

Maybe we set our compass for happiness and then flow with more ease through our daily lives, finding meaning and purpose and joy across all the opportunities that daily life affords. With all the people we interact with and in all the locations where life takes place.

We mine for the gold of meaning, purpose, and joy in our homes, at the office, even on a Saturday afternoon at Home Depot picking up gardening supplies. We take a few minutes for mindfulness in those different locations because we want the feeling of presence. We reach out to people in all those places because we want the feeling of connection. And in tuning in to that mindful mode, the office, your kitchen, your church, the gym, your kid's school, your mother-in-law's home all become simply the locations where your life is expressed. Like different sets in a blockbuster movie starring you. Because it's *your* movie, you are writing and directing, and you never want to lose sight of the bigger story you're creating. One life. Your life. The life of your dreams.

12

Now You See Him,
Now You Don't

Come back. Even as a shadow. Even as a dream.

—Euripides

No one else is on the road. It's early and freezing on this December Saturday morning. The drive will take just over an hour from my apartment in Chicago. I wish it would take forever so that I never arrive. "How strange," I think. As if spending the rest of my life in this car would be better than what I am about to face, but somehow it is. That is my current state. I am feeling two opposite things: numb to my core and powerfully agitated. I can't stop remembering.

*   *   *

In my mind's eye, I see him standing in front of me in his little pull-on jeans, a T-shirt soaked in drool, and with tiny blue lace-up tennis shoes on his feet. He's eighteen months old, his hair is blond and curly, and he so wants to please. It's as if he knows he's here at home with us on a tryout and the grand prize is a family. He rolls down our backyard hill, somersault after somersault. We clap and clap, which fuels the fun. He keeps going until he tuckers out. I wonder why all four of my grandparents have rushed to the house, why my aunts and uncles are stopping by. Seems like we're having a party, though I'm not sure why. Later that night, my dad tucks me in and says maybe this little boy named Johnny could become my brother.

Dad says it will be entirely my decision. Totally up to me. I fall asleep pondering his gentle suggestions, awed by my own power. A brother. The next morning I wake up and creep into the third bedroom, where there is already a crib installed and the little boy is crying and holding his arms in the air. He only wants to come to me. Fresh from sleep, he is suddenly afraid of the big people, the ones Mom and Dad's size. He is desperate for my arms around him. I pull him from the crib, and he clings to me as if his life depends on it. I am soaked in tears and a wet diaper. It is a very long time before he lets me put him down. The deal is sealed.

I am eight years old.

* * *

My memory jumps to a rainy day in May 2009. We are at John's house in Winthrop Harbor, Illinois. He is a forty-two-year-old man now and a father of four children: his namesake, Johnny; daughter, Katie; and little boys Grayson and Cole. We sit around his kitchen table—my brother, his wife, Jodi, and I— drinking coffee and colas. He is nervous, and I feel nauseous. He's waiting for me to give him the report from the detective I hired. I don't think it's the news he's hoping for, but then again I'm not totally sure what's in his heart. He has been utterly silent on this issue with me.

My little brother was told he was adopted as soon as he began asking those "Did I come from your tummy, Mommy?" questions. It was the late sixties, and while probably some family therapy would have been helpful in navigating such a huge issue in a little boy's life, nobody we knew of in the suburbs went to therapy back then, except for the desperately mentally ill.

I never said it out loud, but I had a feeling all was not right in his inner world. I recognized the shaky self-worth because it felt familiar. I could intuit that he had serious struggles with feeling good enough, with his place in the world, with his place in our family. It's what I now think of as the mortal adoption wound. Not every adoptee falls victim, but when they do, it's major.

Destructive patterns emerge and rule the day, the first being

"I was discarded like garbage by the very people who brought me into this world, which makes me unlovable and worthless." And the other, reserved for dark, unhappy days, "Maybe there are fabulous, understanding people out there who are looking for me, and my life would be so much better if I were back in the bosom of my 'real' family." Either way, in my experience as the observant "not-adopted" sister, it is a disease of massive unfinished business, a cauldron of negativity to draw from and frame one's stories about oneself.

Finally, we were grown, and after a few offers on my part and the shake of his head in response, he had Jodi reach out and ask me to help him find his birth family. From the fragmented memories of my little-girl self, I pieced together the facts I overheard during those initial adoption days. He had been found in Lake County, Illinois, when worried neighbors called the authorities. He was with an elderly couple not related to him, and there were signs of neglect. He was born in Chattanooga, Tennessee, on December 26, 1966. His birth name was Johnny Eugene and his last name began with an *M*.

I hired a detective. A few days later, she called me and told me she had spoken to her go-to file clerks, who had browsed the sealed legal records and delivered the goods.

Now, I am sitting next to John at his kitchen table, bracing him for what I've learned. There is no information about his birth mother, who seems to have gone missing. All that's known is that she apparently had an affair with his birth father, and John was born from that union. His birth father died ten years ago of a sudden heart attack. So I have no birth-parent reunion with which to gift him. But there are surviving adult children—his half siblings—including an older sister to whom the detective has spoken personally. They had known about his birth, saw him when he was a baby, and have been wondering what in the world ever happened to him.

As I share the findings, John suddenly lowers his head to the kitchen table, and a torrent of emotion erupts. He chokes with sobs like I've never seen him do before, even as a child. He is, in many ways, a tender soul, but this is primal. Jodi and I weep silently with him and hold the space. She knows something I do not: that even the mention of one birth relative wondering what happened to him is enough.

I reach out my hand and place it on his back. He purges and purges his terrible imaginings and a thousand days' worth of ugly stories he has told himself. I feel protective. I ask him if he wants me to make the first overture to the people in Tennessee. He nods. He wants his big sister to introduce him to his birth family.

* * *

I'm on the Edens Expressway now—the highway that will take me north. I pass the towns of Skokie, Highland Park,

Wilmette, Winnetka, Lake Forest, Libertyville, and even though I would give anything to avoid the task ahead, I keep going.

My memory jumps from the kitchen table to a few months later. John has just returned from a trip to Tennessee with Jodi and the kids to meet those new brothers and sisters. His face looks different to me, as if having those answers has released him from a chronic pain that he's been carrying since I can remember. It's a pain I'd grown so accustomed to that I'd no longer noticed it. But I can see it's gone now. He unpacks new revelations with me. He says he now knows that fate intervened and he was in a way "saved" from a very hard life. The life his half siblings have shared with him in detail has made that clear to him. He plans to continue to get to know them and maybe even find a way to help them. His generosity shines first in every situation. He'd give you the shirt off his back even if it was the only one he owned. He tells me he can't believe how lucky he was to find his way to us.

The whole thing turns out to be the blessing we didn't know we needed. We bask in the glow of healing and a sense of wholeness that follows this massive release of darkness. We manage to avoid the pointless "Why didn't we do this sooner?" recriminations. It's a happy and memorable summer.

The movie in my mind skips ahead a few months. It's October. We're celebrating my fiftieth birthday at a swanky downtown Chicago restaurant. My brother and Jodi toast me with such poignancy that my guests are weeping into their napkins. The playlist has been specially curated by one of my dearest friends. John twirls me around the room to the classic Drifters tune "Save the Last Dance for Me." The photos are glorious, and I know our mom is particularly pleased that we finally have some good ones of our family. Together.

*   *   *

The music from that love bomb of a night fades in my mind. That was just sixty days ago, I note, and I reluctantly come back to the present. The road is moving swiftly under the tires of my Range Rover, familiar strip malls rush by to my left and to my right, and soon I am farther into the country and I see the trees I know so well. Just ahead is the exit that leads to my destination. I have about five minutes left to prepare myself for a task that is unthinkable. I'm not ready.

I pull up to the second house my mom and dad have ever owned, on a wooded hill down the street from a pretty lake. In the thirty years they've lived here, I've made this drive so often, escaping the city for family picnics, holidays, dinners. John and his kids always meet me here.

I look at my watch. I gather myself. There is snow on the ground. I'll have to be careful when I get out of the car because it's probably slippery as is usual at this time of year.

I know Mom and Dad are up early—Dad having his coffee, tea for Mom; they're probably doing a bit of last-minute wrapping of their swap gifts for our annual Salata Cousins Christmas celebration, set for later in the afternoon. Dad is no doubt watching the birds in the backyard in his normal morning-glory "cheerified" fashion. They are happy, and in a matter of minutes I will say the words that will make happiness impossible.

My eyes take in the wooden steps leading to the top of the hill. I wonder if I can make myself walk up them. The only thing that may possibly power me is knowing that this task is better done by me than by anyone else on the planet. I have a fleeting thought, "How does one do a terrible thing well?" I open the car door and begin to climb. I am steps away from their front door, which I know will be open because it always is. I take one last breath and review my mission.

I must tell them their son is dead.

Then I must help them survive that news.

* * *

I cross the threshold. My mom sees me first. Her face breaks into a big smile, delighted and surprised to find me in her house at this hour. Her smile lessens as she has a moment to take in my face, my eyes, the raw grief I am holding back like Moses and the parted sea. She keeps her now-worried eyes on me and calls for my dad. I ask them to sit on either side of me. I grasp their hands in mine.

I open my heart as wide as I can and I say the words I'll never be able to take back. Words I know will ruin their lives.

"He must have had a heart attack in his sleep. Jodi woke up and found him gone. She called me. I came here to you as fast as I could."

I cannot bear the time it takes to register. I break inside watching their faces crumple, the impact felt. I have another fleeting thought: "I'm in the midst of the worst moment of my life, having experienced its runner-up just ninety minutes earlier."

Jodi arrives, ghostly pale, in shock. We sit on the couch and fiercely hold hands. I say to her, "Let's just breathe. Let's just breathe." We sit there for what feels like hours. There is nothing to hold on to but presence. We are incapable of anything but stillness. It occurs to me as I hear people crying in the background, nose-blowing, murmured conversations, that this is love.

The mess of this moment. The unsteadiness of it all; the wearing off of shock and the heating up of pain. The sinking pit of it and the swollen eyes of it. The coffee made. The lunch brought in that no one can eat. The sick-to-our-stomachs feeling. The waves of "Oh my Gods." The "poor kids" remarks. Love. All of it.

I do the human thing and recall the last time I spoke to him, Thursday night. He had been helping our dad through a broken-arm crisis. Taking him to physical therapy every day. Spending more time at Mom and Dad's in a few short weeks than he had throughout the whole previous year. He was in this very house when we spoke on the phone. Dad had hollered after him from the front door to come back and say hello to me. John was probably tired and just wanted to get home to Jodi and the kids, but he came back inside anyway. I acknowledged his goodness on our call and told him he was Dad's guardian angel. "What a wonder," I think, as I ponder all of the final synchronicities. We signed off from our last chat in this life-time as per usual: "Love you, Juan." "Love you more, Sher." And just like that, he's gone.

*   *   *

For these six years since, I have rarely revisited that day. I think that maybe it will kill me to relive it. But in my middle-of-life quest to leave no drawer of my psyche unopened, I sit here alone in front of a fire and make myself remember the tiniest of details. My phone ringing at 7:30 a.m.—unusually early for a Saturday. Jodi trying to get out the words to make me understand. The drive. The rest of the day. And the days that followed.

I watch how we force ourselves to rise from our sleepless beds and bathe and dress and eat a few forkfuls of grief casseroles and keep going. I see us pulling off a week of Christmas and Santa stuff for the little boys while behind the scenes we meet at the funeral home and plan the memorial. I see me pick up the phone to dial John's newly found birth family to tell them their miraculous reunion was also goodbye. I see myself sitting at my own kitchen island the night before, asking the Universe, asking John, to help me write the words that will eulogize him and ease this pain for everyone left behind. The words come, but they are a balm only for the surface blow. Everybody will have to dig deep in their own way for healing. Cry their own tears. Scream into their own pillows.

Except me. I see myself put that personal healing piece on pause. We are in crisis mode. I am a producer, and this terrible new reality for my family must be produced for our survival. There are financial details, school for the kids, emotional support for Jodi, and check-ins with Mom and Dad twice daily and each weekend for a very long time. That will be my second full-time job as I head back to work at *The Oprah Winfrey Show*. The holiday hiatus is over. And things will ramp up to warp speed fast. We've got a show to do. I watch myself on autopilot employ an unconscious survival strategy that seems to make some kind of sense even as I review it now. I will put every cell of my body, every thought and every feeling on active high alert so I won't ever get ambushed like this again.

I walk through my life that way for the next six years.

*   *   *

And yet, it never works, does it? Sweeping the heart-crushing storm under the rug, then taking up our position at the gate to stand guard with a watchful eye for the next disaster. Because once you get whacked to the core, you know that even worse things are possible. You are no longer one of the lucky ones who remain unscathed by tragedy.

I go back to my reckoning and see the pieces of it tied to this cataclysmic event, in my life. I see the ways I've traded intimacy for impenetrability. How I've comforted myself with external things and avoided the internal fire walking that's required to heal this wound. To let the pain take me to its depths so I can let it go. How I told myself a bunch of crazy-making stories that I was in charge of everyone's recovery and ultimate happiness, that I could help save them all even as I remained unsaved.

Not true. Not true. I see it now; all that is just not true.

We must save ourselves. That's what my present knowing tells me. We must brave all of our unfelt griefs, or we will spend the second half of our lives dragging those joy-stealing anchors into every relationship, every job, every moment of every single day we have left, and we will never know how happy, how content, how satisfied we might have been. Our lives become less inhabited when we freeze our hearts to avoid pain. And tragically we end up marching inside the skin of our unlived lives right to the bitter end. I don't want to end up that way. Blocked. Self-protected. Frozen. And my brother wouldn't want that for me either.

So I decide to let the waves of awful crash over me. I cry and I cry until I feel empty. The reservoir of grief refills and empties, refills, and empties . . . and still there's more.

Finally, wrecked and exhausted, I excavate from deep in my center the buried gem that has been quietly waiting to be discovered. John has led me to a treasure. His sudden magician-like disappearance from our physical world, which I have carried as my greatest loss, might be the bread crumbs on the path leading to my most valuable gain. The knowing that will transform me: I will *dream* my life as if I will live to be one hundred. I will *live* my life as if this day—the day I wake up in—is the only one I get.

I ease myself back into the warm water of my bath. And I cry and I cry and I cry . . .

13

Kissy the Underdog

*She is telling me that she came into the world
on a mission to work with you specifically so
she can share some very important lessons.*

—Nancy Windheart, renowned animal communicator

I n the mysterious and intriguing world of animal communication, Nancy Windheart is considered world class. As
we begin our ninety-minute phone reading, her voice is full
of kindness as she goes right to work telling me what my two
dogs, Kissy and Bella, really think about their lives with me.
We are in for a rollicking, otherworldly ride.

Frankly, I had been at my wits' end and more than a little
scared about Kissy's failing eyesight when Nancy Windheart's
name came up in conversation several times with different
people. I think of these kinds of coincidences as signs, and I

usually follow them like cairns on a trail to mostly valuable outcomes.

There was a notice on her website that she was not taking appointments, but the Universe intervened, and somehow I got behind the digital wall and accidentally paid for a consultation. Nancy was nice enough to honor the request instead of just refunding my money.

In preparation, I sent her two photos, one of Bella, my then-nine-year-old English bulldog, and one of Bella's biological mother, Kissy, my then-eleven-year-old English bulldog. Kissy had recently had her seventh surgery since she'd joined my little family eight years before. A deep ulcer in her eye had required a graft, but the alternative was removing the eyeball altogether. Once home, she was totally blind during the recovery phase, and she was very upset and disoriented by her new circumstances. We were both beside ourselves as she charged into walls, crumpling her protective cone. I feebly tried to anticipate her next move, acting as her "seeing eye human" while wringing my hands and silently panicking.

So now I'm hoping Nancy Windheart can help. She begins by describing Kissy: "She's strong, stubborn, and very clear about what she wants." (So far, on the money.) She goes on to say that Kissy can't see much right now but notes I am being careful with her so she won't hurt herself. She says that Kissy loves her life and the only thing that could make it better would be more treats, and more time with her human, meaning me. (I have often thought that Kissy would literally eat herself to death if I allowed unlimited meals. She also knows where I am every moment I am in the house, like a personal tracking device, and when I am gone, she waits forlornly by the door for hours.)

Kissy reveals to Nancy that Bella annoys her much of the time with her sparkly, silly energy and that I am her deepest, truest love, her soul mate. She reveals that she and I were supposed to rendezvous in this life. Most important, she wants me to know that her difficult beginnings were important so that she could become the gift she wanted to be for me.

*   *   *

In 2010, the year Kissy came into my world, life was a bit of a blur. I was reeling from the shock and awe of what I think of as the Holiday Horribilis. The previous December 19, the morning of our annual Salata Cousins Christmas, my younger brother didn't wake up. He had suffered a massive heart attack in his sleep.

The days that followed were like a crazy nightmare during which you walk through water but never get anywhere. Between contending with all of our broken hearts and the enormity of my job, I had no room for one more thing in my life.

But one morning that spring, I woke up from a dream with a powerful and inexplicable urge to check in with the Oklahoma dog breeder from whom I had gotten Bella. From time to time, I had thought about getting another puppy (maybe even a little biological sibling for Bella), but there was no way on earth I could take that on in the middle of what I was facing.

For those who do it well, puppy training is serious business. If you don't rigorously commit to the crate training method, you'll be living in a virtual litter box for years to come. Bella had arrived at eleven weeks old, and despite my intense work schedule at the show, it was my sacred vow to do her training right. For several months I slept in sweatpants, set my alarm, scooped her up every two to three hours from her crate next to the bed, and headed down the elevator of my vintage apartment in Lincoln Park. I would then set her on the grass in the middle of the night, do the "yay potty" dance when she was finished, and off we'd go back upstairs until the alarm went off again.

I also wanted her to have confidence in other dogs and in humans, so socialization was high on my priority list. She went to agility school, along with tons of classmates, and came with me almost everywhere I went. My herculean efforts were rewarded. Bella was indeed a perfectly potty-trained, very happy girl who loved all creatures great and small and who could literally stop traffic.

Our walks around Lincoln Park were a riot. Cars would pull over, and admirers would jump out and ask to snap photos of Bella on their smartphones. She loved her celebrity status, often refusing to go inside until she had finished greeting her public. She had an odd quirk of needing to be noticed by at least five strangers (her quota) before she was content to end our walk and go back home. At 5:00 in the morning this was sometimes difficult. I would desperately call out to passersby, "Please say hi to her! I have to get to work!"

When I had the weird dream about the breeder, I went to their website to see the latest news. Across the home page was a huge banner: SELLING ALL OF OUR FEMALES. For the rest of the day a thought floated in and out of my mind: "Was Bella's mother in that group?" On Bella's AKC registration her mom's name was listed as Hershey's Country Kiss, and her nickname was Kissy. Then another thought: "Who do you sell breeding females to? Another breeder?" I felt compelled to call and find out.

When the woman answered, I introduced myself as a former customer, reminded her of Bella, and asked why she was selling all the girls. It turned out there had been a sickness in her family and the females took a lot of care, which she couldn't manage as she would be out of town for most of the year. I then inquired about Bella's mother. The woman said that Kissy had already been purchased by a woman who was starting a little breeding operation in her backyard.

Da Dum. Da Da Da Dummmm.

The ominous drumbeat of destiny sounded in my head with

that bit of odious news. English bulldogs are very difficult to breed. They must always be born by a C-section because their heads are too large to pass through the birth canal—one of the side effects of selective breeding. So this was not the kind of dog for a novice "wannabe breeder" just starting up a business "in her backyard." Over the next two days, I casually mentioned these facts to my dog-loving friends, who all grimaced, while one made an emotional plea. He said, "You have to do this. I can't get that dog out of my mind. You have to take her, Sheri. She is supposed to be with you and Bella."

Even though that idea was *ridiculous*, considering my current circumstances, the fate of Kissy—the four-year-old English bulldog in the middle of Oklahoma, on whom I had never laid eyes—was haunting me.

I called the breeder back. "Ma'am, I want to adopt Kissy; please say it's not too late."

"Well, honey, she is promised to someone else," came the reply.

"Look, I know I'm right about this. It's what's supposed to happen. I will pay any price to get her, and you can trust that she will have the best possible life with me," I promised. (Where this conviction was coming from I really can't say, because the idea was still completely outlandish.)

"Let me talk to my husband," she said.

The next morning when we spoke she said they had prayed

about it, and they agreed that Kissy would be better off with me and Bella and they wouldn't raise the price. I wired them $2,500, and oh, by the way, Kissy was to arrive at O'Hare airport in two days.

So it was happening, whether I could handle this new addition to my family or not. Kissy was coming.

* * *

I had done this drill before. I remembered standing at the American Airlines dog-arrival area when the "puppy stork" dropped off Bella. It was a glorious day. She was like a little stuffed animal—an eleven-pound darling—sporting a pink bow and a necklace of plastic white pearls, and she was only slightly traumatized by her travels. Once we were in the car on the journey home, she promptly laid her head on my shoulder and fell fast asleep; she remained in that position for much of the day. Picture perfect.

Kissy's arrival was something else altogether.

The first thing I noticed as I approached her travel crate was an overpowering barnyard stench. I opened the door and the pitiful creature inside stirred, but she clearly had no intention of leaving her poop-filled cave. I pulled and tugged and got my first look at her.

My heart beat wildly as I considered what was happening. I now had a real farm animal on my hands, not someone's former

pet who'd been outgrown and needed rescue, but a real out-
doors kind of being who freaked out over a variety of things:
shiny tile floors, the opening of elevator doors, any sudden
noises she hadn't heard before (like crackling paper), and walking on a leash (she flat-out refused). And did I mention her
twelve saggy boobs were literally dragging on the ground?

I sprang into producer mode. We were miles from the car,
so this was going to happen in little increments. I hoisted up
her forty-five-pound body and began to walk as far and fast as
I could. Then I'd set her down and we'd rest and I'd gather my
breath. Then we'd go again, my friend and me switching off.
It seemed to take forever, but eventually we were at my car in
the airport parking lot.

We spoke nary a word as he drove us home. We were all
in shock. I held Kissy in the back seat as I tried not to vomit.
She was terrified, panting uncontrollably and stinking to high
heaven of manure. But I was overcome. I had a sense that she
had faced her deepest fears to get to me and that she might be
the bravest soul I had ever encountered. I leaned down and
made forever kinds of promises in gentle whispers, "I will
always be here for you, and I will always take care of you.
Everything is going to be all right." And then I cried a little.
This was going to be a long, long road for both of us, and I
had no idea how we were going to get through it. When we finally got to my apartment, the mother-daughter reunion I had

anticipated fell flat as a pancake as Bella took one sniff of her long-lost mama, turned up her nose, and walked into the next room as disinterested as I'd ever seen her. Not a good sign.

We began Kissy's rehab with a well-deserved hysterectomy and moved on from there to her first eye surgery, multiple-teeth pulling, a single mastectomy for a tumor, a splenectomy, and the removal of various growths. She was the most stoic patient I had ever seen, behaving as if to say, "Get on with it! Let's get this part over and done with." I did naively inquire about a little plastic surgery on the remaining udder-like appendages that still dragged on the floor, but when I saw the vet's expression, I knew it was a stupidly awful question that only the worst kind of person would ask.

Over time, her body would take on a new shape as I took charge of her health and spent every cent I made on her care and well-being, but in those early months, Kissy would stop traffic, too. People would look at me with disgust as their eyes took her in—from head to nipples to toe—as if they were convinced I was running an illicit puppy mill out of my city apartment. But Kissy and I pressed on and tried to hold our heads high.

Kissy's road to domestication was arduous, but her determination to "get it right" was downright inspiring. Even though it seemed to hurt her pride a bit, she'd look to Bella and observe what seemed to be the right doggie behaviors in our little family and then try to execute similar moves. It was a game of reluctant mimicry. I could almost see the sweat on Kissy's brow as she worked these problems out in her mind. How to do this? How to do that? What does Mom like? How do I get some praise? Month after month she kept at it, literally reinventing herself.

*   *   *

Almost eight years and the price of a pied-à-terre in Dubuque later, the transformation has been nothing short of astounding. Kissy's, Bella's, and mine. Mine especially.

Kissy has elicited from me a dedication and commitment I have never known. And I am a pretty dedicated, devoted sort. Although even someone blowing their nose at the dinner table has me gagging, there is nothing too gross, too difficult, too impossible that I won't do for her (and that includes the many exploding-diarrhea episodes, the details of which should and will remain private).

In return, she has loved me as a soul mate and continues to be a living, breathing, daily lesson in unconditional love. She is certainly not the most gorgeous gal by best-in-show stan-dards, but to me she's beautiful beyond all reason. She doesn't have the warmest personality, but I find her mesmerizing and completely irresistible. She snores, she farts, she blows snot in my mouth when I bend down to kiss her (yes, quite gross, I know), and she couldn't care less if anyone but me likes her or not. She is in no rush to win a stranger's heart. So of course, she's the one for whom people stand on their heads. I watch with complete amusement and total understanding as they act like fools to gain her trust, affection, or just even a moment of attention and connection. Bella is in the bag. Easy-breezy. Kissy is another story.

* * *

I don't know if other pet moms and dads do this, but I find myself practicing my babies' impending deaths as the ultimate loin-girding exercise. It's a strange, strange thing to be in a deep relationship with another sentient being who literally arrives with an expiration date that seems to come as quickly as that on a carton of sour cream. A being who is here and gone in the briefest of years. In fact, if you have pets throughout your lifetime, you are guaranteed a multitude of painful, wrenching goodbyes.

English bulldogs generally have a life span of eight to twelve years, at the outside, they say. Kissy has passed the upper statistical limit and Bella is right behind her. I can't imagine a moment without them—they are so rooted in my experience now. I practice their deaths so I don't get caught unawares by yet another incapacitating grief. These sessions, which begin with my imagining the concept of them dead, are searingly painful, and as I become almost hysterical, I think, "This is ridiculous, stop it right now" and pull myself back. But secretly, I know I am toughening myself up for an eventuality that is just part of the deal with this kind of love.

So I hold them close and smell their ears and kiss their eyelids and stay so fully in the present that I will never forget the feel of them. The softness of their temples, the way they nudge me to say hello, how their tummies feel as I rub them. How they love a little peanut butter treat every night at 8:30 sharp. How Kissy stares into my eyes from across the room for what seems like hours. These days, I feel as if my soul-mate girl is slowly getting us both ready for our farewell.

I would never have believed that the farm animal in that crate at O'Hare had the makings of a Buddha, yet Kissy has become one of my greatest teachers. She struggled to learn new things and adopt new ways, and she mastered them (mostly). She endured lots of medical interventions so that she could thrive (just like me). She's every bit as transformed by her efforts as I am by mine, and then some. Even now, as I tweak my recipe for the life of my dreams, there are, of course, days when my middle-of-life reinvention feels like a big mountain I still have yet to summit and moments of frustration when I find it all too much. But then I think of my sweet underdog who willed herself to my door and then, step-by-step, made herself over for her love of me and her dream of a life in the civilized world. And I am inspired. And recommitted.

In the hallowed days of the famed *Oprah* show makeover, we chose viewers who wanted to change their looks, their homes, or any part of their lives and brought in the best of the best experts to primp, renovate, and remodel. We had a time-tested formula for presenting the guests and their stories to garner the biggest audience possible. Segment One was the beginning of the show, which was prime real estate: strictly reserved for the showstopper, the standing O, the most amazing "after."

That's how I think of my Kissy girl. Segment One, for sure.

Kissy's Rules for a Happy Life

* Don't be a yes girl.

* Just say no. A lot.

* Take time to smell the . . . well, anything.

* Who cares what anyone thinks!

* You deserve lots and lots of treats.

* You can never take too many naps.

* Find your tribe and don't let them out of your sight.

* And last and most important, no matter how you begin, you can always have a happy ending.

* * *

Author's note: On August 30, 2019, my Kissy girl crossed the rainbow bridge.

Her departure at 13½ years old was agony and grace. Right to her last breath, she loved me ferociously. She had made it her life's purpose.

And she honored my one request of her. "Let me know when you are ready, my love, don't make me worry and wonder." That morning she let me know. It was unmistakable.

It was time.

And the Universe went to work. In my purse was a card that a stranger had given me at a book-signing event for *The Beautiful No* just seven days before. The lovely woman who had come to hear me read said, "This is for Kissy." On the card was the name of a vet who spends her life helping puppies ease on over to the other side. I called. She had one spot open before the Labor Day holiday. She would arrive at 1:00 p.m.

We had four hours left, and we spent them snuggling and eating more treaties than I usually would allow—all the treaties I could find in the house. How many kisses could I fit in during our last hours together in physical form? Normally she would have been napping but not that morning. She was alert, peering at me, listening intently to my words of love and thanks. Bella circled us, sensing that something serious was going on. Wanting to know but not wanting to know. I understood. Their wise good-manners teacher from back in our Chicago days had given me sage advice. Miss Bridgit said: "Make sure Bella knows Kissy has transitioned. Don't let her wonder why she disappeared."

In the hands of the traveling vet with a heart of gold, Kissy's passing was ease-filled. The only pain was mine.

14

Anatomy of a Rut

Buon giorno, Professore Patrick. Me chiamo Sheri.
Sono studentessa di Italiano. Sono di Chicago. Piacere.

—Me, Italian class, 2018

It is month eight of my Italian lessons, and I am burning it up. I can now announce my name and say "nice to meet you." Anything more will require a cumbersome study of my dog-eared notes and cheat sheets. In a group class that fluctuates in size and convenes every Tuesday at noon, I am the least skilled. Read: the worst. And surprisingly, as an overachiever, I feel no shame at my incompetence, just sheer delight. When I walk out of the classroom into the open air, my brain feels as if it's been scrambled alive. And I love it. I am officially moving out of a rut.

We all do it.

We don't mean to but we do.

We accidentally get routinized.

We do the same things, the same ways, over and over.

Like our regular drives to and from places.

Our same grocery store.

Our daily schedules.

Cook.

Clean.

Shower.

Dress.

Go to work.

Come home.

Undress.

Eat.

Watch TV.

Tidy.

Sleep.

Ugh. No wonder we lose interest in our own lives.

To some extent, big or small, so many of us feel emotionally dulled and unenthusiastic, and we aren't sure why. Especially in the middle of life, aka the been-there-done-that era. The insidious thing about living in a rut is that you may not have a clue you are in one until the occasional wild twist of fate forces your eyeballs up over the edge of its canyon-y sides. And once you smell that fresh air and see the new sights up there, you gasp with amazement at how much better the experience of living could be. "Why did it take me so long to pop my head up?" you wonder.

A rut, to my way of thinking, is a second cousin twice removed from mild depression—another dank pool I've taken a swim in more than once. Years ago, I concluded that I descend from a long line of women on my maternal side who suffered from intermittent low-grade depression. (Mind you, this is according to no one but me.) I saw the gloom descend on my mom and her mom and the older aunties even as they tried hard to keep it at bay. It was never debilitating enough to completely sideline any of us, but it was, let's say, "a thing." For me, it was the optimism thief. It would come over me out of nowhere, and I would feel like I was slowly sinking in my chair. This gray cloud loved carbs, despair, and the endless repeating of doom-laden stories while it added a muddled tinge to everything in my gaze. I'd power my way through each "episode" with an effective distraction—a mountain of busyness. Then, one morning, I'd awaken and feel kinda sunny. It had passed.

My mom dealt with her own depressive stints by keeping her house neat as a pin, getting fully dressed every single day, and putting on a bright coral-colored lipstick. She abhorred the "full nap," where you actually lie down with a blanket, and allowed herself only the closing of her eyes while she leaned back in our one comfy chair in the den. She was a foil to every bit of midday respite and sleepy self-care I would attempt. "Keep moving" was the only cure she knew. She'd let me sleep in for a hangover but not for a bit of sadness.

Throughout my very fast-paced stint in television, I didn't allow myself much time to ruminate over how I was feeling. Everything emotionally challenging was to be powered through for the greater good—our mission of putting out life-changing content for a worldwide audience. Yet even at a company like Harpo Studios, where making dreams come true for people was a daily event, I was still able to dig some crater-size ruts. Which goes to show that the defining trait of any rut is the *sameness*. You may be living pretty happily, but without mixing it up, things get stale.

Like millions in the workforce, I'd been in staff jobs working for others since leaving college. That meant all weekdays were claimed by my employer, and my work time would often spill over to the weekends as well. Once I stepped off that train to work for myself, I felt like E.T. the extraterrestrial as I explored Mondays through Fridays, a newly discovered land. I found a bustling world of goings-on. Coffee shops packed with freelancers holding midmorning meetings. Lunch spots populated with writers and business builders all intensely tuned in to their laptop virtual offices. Off I went to my neighborhood bank to introduce myself to the tellers. I was giddy that I would know their names and they mine. I took little notice that they seemed less excited about our budding friendships.

Slowly, as my energy rose and my enthusiasm for daily life seemed to bubble up, I could see that I was coming out of a routinized way of living. It had all been self-created, which was good because that meant I could fix it.

I began with daily travel. Living in a sprawling city like L.A., known for monumental traffic snarls, I couldn't get from here to there without the navigational app called Waze. Lo and behold, turns out Waze is a world-class rut buster. There is nary a chance you will be directed the same way twice in a week, so right there you're assured that you'll be taking a new route every time you leave the house. In Chicago, I'd driven the exact same route to work every single day for a decade. Now, driving unexplored paths was a wonderful start to a new life.

I looked for more ways to add "new" to my middle-of-life experience. Along with learning Italian, I began to tick things off my someday list.

Back in junior high, I had been a member of the Royal Christie Ski Club. In those northern-suburb-of-Chicago winters, I'd board a yellow bus on Saturday mornings and be driven to icy Wisconsin mountains where the skiers who couldn't make it to the powder out west plied their sport. In all the years since, I had never made it back to the slopes, but

I kept the dream alive with casual mentions here and there. Now, in a major rut-transcending move, I planned a ski weekend with my friend and business partner Nancy to celebrate her fifty-second birthday. Just making the reservations and buying some outdoor gear felt madcap. The energy we were stirring up together felt next level, and we were dizzy with excitement.

We loaded up my car and laughed all the way to Mammoth, California, five hours north. Our lodge was adorable—legend had it this was where John Wayne and his movie-star buddies had liked to lie low. They particularly liked the bar and the fireplace. Same for us!

Our first view of the mountains the next morning put a damper on our giddy moods. Tentatively, we made our way to the rental hut from the parking lot, feeling like bundled-up stiff-legged kids. Those craggy peaks in the distance were *huge* and slippery-looking, much higher than I remembered. Suddenly, we were all too aware of my knee pain and Nancy's sore ankle. This was madness.

Wisely, we had hired an instructor for the day so we wouldn't be on our own. We were told to meet her at the foot of the learners' area. But before that, we would have to revisit some painful territory. My God, putting on ski boots for the first time in decades is not only a sweaty struggle but torturous. And the throbbing of your shins when you walk! The awkwardness in taking giant clodhopper steps as you swing your legs to and fro. How had I forgotten all of this? A walk that normally should have taken seven minutes required a full twenty-five with a couple breaks thrown in to regroup. Along the way I'd eyeball those dangly, dangerous-looking chairlifts visible in the distance. Knowing that the goal was to be sitting in one of them in less than an hour, *yikes* was coursing through my veins.

We were late to our designated meetup—the automated moving carpet known in the olden days as the bunny hill. Our oldest cohort was five. The disparity between this little incline and that mammoth mountain the instructor intended to introduce us to was chilling. "Absolutely no way," I thought. And who knew so much had changed in my absence from this sport? For example: turns out the basic life-saving maneuver that had rescued me many a time had been completely renamed.

"Do the pizza! Do the pizza!" the instructor would shout. What? What happened to "snow plowing"? To my way of thinking, this was highly undignified for anyone old enough to drive.

Happily, our graceful and also fiftysomething instructor was well versed in the shaky-ski-leg syndrome that affects middle-of-lifers who return to the hills, and she whisked us up the mountain before we could race back to the lodge for toddies. Soon we were flying and laughing and screaming with delight as we went up and down and pizza'd our way through the day. We were doing something brave and exciting and different. Our newfound joy extended for hours in front of a blazing fire as we recounted story after story of how we'd conquered those slopes like Olympians.

Once home, I returned to my alchemy; spinning my bucket list into gold with renewed verve. What other experiences had I been saving up for the right time that never came?

I soon found one that had been percolating since way back in Chicago, before my start at *Oprah*. I would eyeball the cooking-class offerings at Sur La Table downtown, and my eyes would linger on the description of their signature Knife Skills Class. I wanted to learn once and for all how to properly chop things like carrots, celery, bell peppers, onions, and so on. I wanted to learn how to slice and dice with the kind of ease and speed that would allow me to whip up menus that felt life-giving. Over the years, many a good-cook friend had tried to teach me how to wield a proper chef's knife in the kitchen, but without practice, my new learnings would never quite stick.

Now, in my commitment to bring some newness to my life, I signed up for the Knife Skills Class at the L.A. Farmers Market Sur La Table store. This time, I followed through. I showed up, met my fellow students, my fabulous teacher Chef Gill, and his trusty sous chefs. I was corrected many, many times with kindness and affection, but I kept at it. In the end, I was one of the least accomplished of all, yet I cared not one iota. I chopped carrots, celery, and green peppers awkwardly but thoroughly. Then I took my turn at the actual pot and stirred, braised, and simmered each recipe we prepared. I observed my classmates as they took their turn at the knife, and I learned from those demonstrations. Then we wrapped our class by tasting our dishes comprised of our cooked choppings and cheered one another for our successes. I was happy when I walked in and super-charged as I packed up to go. In the teaching kitchen, I snapped a selfie so I'd remember the feeling.

When I got home and studied that picture, I identified the look on my face as *fresh joy*, the palpable feeling you get when you have deliberately brought the feeling of newness back into your life. I was bright-eyed, with a new perspective, a new skill, a "newness" spilling out of every pore. There's nothing quite like that marriage of adventure and discovery. (Plus, now I can look a big fat green pepper in the eye and know I can make something good-looking out of it with a finely honed blade of steel.)

Adding to the mix was the fact that I had done what I said I was going to do. I am celebrating over just that. Ten times that Saturday morning I thought about canceling because there seemed to be more urgent things that needed my time. But I didn't.

Our earliest days in this life are filled with new experiences because we are, in fact, new to being human. Then we are new to marriage or partnership. To careering. To mothering, fathering, or other popular life tracts. What I am discovering at this stage of life is that there aren't going to be a whole lot of "new" things showing up at my doorstep to surprise me. I will have to take charge of making sure the life force keeps on flowing by creating opportunities for adventuring, learning, discovering.

And adventure is not a one-note song. It's not just climbing mountains (though I would dearly love to summit Kili), or jumping out of airplanes (did it, and *never* again), or white-water-rafting down the Alps (fell out of the boat and conked my head). Not just the daring escapades but a lane much wider and more welcoming. It is just about *new*. That is what we are trying to awaken in our lives. Learning about wine, speaking French or Italian or Polish, knitting a scarf, playing the ukulele, practicing kundalini yoga, attending the symphony—it doesn't matter what it is as long it's unfamiliar territory.

So let us fire up our inner Waze apps, I say, and reroute the well-worn grooves in our neural pathways. Let's pledge to mix things up but good. We'll charge into strange places and situations with dust flying. Stir up spicy new dreams with our imaginations ablaze. Double dose ourselves with fresh joy as if our very lives depend on it.

I think I want to learn the tango.

15

Thanksgiving Redux

If you would just decide to play the game
of appreciation on a regular basis, you
would live happily ever after.

—Abraham-Hicks

I have unleashed a powerful practice that may elevate my life forever and connect me in new and deeper ways to my family. After freeing myself of convention, a predictably delicious menu of a dozen dishes, and my own deeply rooted expectations, I took my most favorite holiday and gave it a massive overhaul.

But look at that, I am ahead of the story.

It begins as a Thanksgiving tale, rooted in ninety years of tradition on my mother's side. Our annual celebrations regularly convened through world wars, the Great Depression, a moon walk, *Seinfeld*, and the invention of the salad spinner. And oh my goodness, how my grandma Annie, my great auntie Mae, my cousins and second cousins, and most especially my mom loved Thanksgiving.

I hail from Waukegan, Illinois, an hour due north of Chicago, and, trust me, the weather during the third week in November is generally a gloomy, leafless, drab, gray affair. We weren't one of those active families that scheduled the *Life* magazine flag football game in the morning. We were more the let's-get-this-party-started kind of group.

We'd set a 3:00 p.m. arrival time, show up with bells on, and then eat and drink our way through 10:00 p.m. or later. The cocktails were poured right from the start, and the appetizers were abundant: gargantuan cheese balls, shrimp cocktail, piping hot artichoke dip, and dozens of deviled eggs graced the coffee tables while football blared on the TV. Around 6:30 p.m., we'd say grace and sit down to our formal china, crystal, sterling silver Thanksgiving dinner.

The menu was pretty much locked. Rare substitutions. Few tweaks. Turkey; dressing; gravy; mashed potatoes; sweet potatoes; mashed rutabaga; oyster stuffing; relish trays loaded with olives, pickles, carrots, and celery; wiggly canned cranberries; green bean casserole; canned corn (for a special green-bean-hating cousin-in-law); Waldorf Cool Whip salad; dinner rolls; pumpkin pie; pecan pie; and lots of aerosol whipped cream (sampled earlier in the kitchen by my cousin Debbi and me straight from the can with great hilarity).

Coffee and cordials were served in family heirloom bone china cups and antique snifters collected over a lifetime or two. We played Trivial Pursuit while sipping specially made Irish Cream coffees, shared stories and updates, and were always left feeling it had been the best Thanksgiving ever. Unlike the holiday that follows in December, Thanksgiving has an ease that I think may have much to do with the absence of presents, with all the expectation and commotion and joy and disappointment they bring. Thanksgiving is about *presence*— it's about being together. Holding new babies. Hanging out in the kitchen for the intense gravy-making ritual with the matriarchs. Having one-on-ones off in the corner where the elders dispense their wisdom to whoever is chosen that year to get "the talk."

My grandma Annie and her sister, my great auntie Mae, traded hosting duties for many decades and then passed it down to my mom and cousin Shirlee and then finally, more decades later, it was mine. Each of those four years I had it, I took half a day Tuesday and Wednesday off from my busy *Oprah* job to prepare. I peeled and chopped and mixed and baked and ultimately finished my chores only minutes before

I opened the door to my twelfth-floor lakefront apartment on Thursday afternoon. Helming a formal sit-down holiday feast for twenty-five to thirty people when you are not a cook requires real pluck, I tell you.

The truth is, my years of hosting Thanksgiving were almost over before they began. The first year, my mom had been undergoing course after course of chemo, so she sat at my kitchen island on Wednesday, carefully instructing me on how to do it all her way, since there was no other way to do it. She made everything better. The next morning, at the crack of dawn, we loaded that thirty-pound stuffed bird into the big oven of my rarely used professional six-burner stove. All of my prep efforts had borne real fruit. My formal tables were set, crystal gleaming, silver shining, casseroles made and ready to be heated up for dinner—nothing to do but relax and get ready to greet my guests. I felt confident. In hindsight, perhaps too confident.

At about 1:30 p.m., a little voice in my head said, "Hmmm. The turkey has been in for hours. Why don't I smell anything?" I walked to the kitchen and opened the door to discover a gigantic, pimply ice-cold bird in my sparkling clean, fancy oven that had clearly malfunctioned—on Thanksgiving.

Mom, Dad, and I tried not to panic, but this was a bona fide disaster. Judging by the time, our guests were out in the suburbs loading up their cars for the seventy-minute jaunt to the city. We knew in our hearts that Thanksgiving without turkey would have been the equivalent of a Charlie Brown Christmas. I could just hear those mournful tones.

Ever the pragmatist, Dad suggested we call everyone and ask them to stop by their local grocery stores and grab some rotisserie chickens.

"Oh no," I thought, "not on my watch."

I tucked my pj's into my Ugg boots, threw on my long winter coat and sunglasses, and drove like the wind to my local Whole Foods Market. God bless them, I will always be grateful that they were truly there for me in my darkest hostessing hour. I ran to the meat counter and spied two trays of sliced herb-roasted turkey breast. A massive mound of white meat would have to suffice. Maybe nobody would notice.

"Those are mine!" I said, frantically calling dibs.

"All of it?" the man behind the counter asked incredulously.

"Yes, good sir, wrap it up—and hurry!" I shrieked.

I also tucked three quarts of Whole Foods gravy under my armpits and ran to the checkout. I got home just seconds before my first guests arrived, jumped in the shower to rinse off the flop sweat, and changed into my holiday outfit. I gave a wink to my mom, who was worried sick, reassured my dad that I had everything under control, and proceeded with my first Thanksgiving dinner ever. I was outed only near the end of the meal when someone asked for a drumstick. I told the story, now legend.

*   *   *

Our lives are bettered by ritual. Ritual makes things matter as it blesses the ordinary and elevates it to extraordinary. Author and teacher Geneen Roth says that the way we do one thing is the way we do all things because in the end we are the "doers." That makes sense. So if we can infuse the sacred into the way we do one small thing, like making a cup of tea, the rest of our lives become richer. By that standard, our deeply ritualized family Thanksgivings were indeed sacred ground.

Those Thursdays in November were the foundation of my family's love story. Generation by generation, we all added chapters to that saga, and with each passing year I like to think that the love grew. Of course, it wasn't about the food; it was always about the people. People who made it a priority to be together on a day that celebrates thankfulness. People who were connected by a tribal sense of belonging to a shared history. For nearly a century, it was something to hold on to when we were buffeted about by the storms of life.

I had imagined I would be hosting our Thanksgiving ritual forever and ever, or at least until I couldn't fit one more person in my house. But then I moved to Los Angeles, and that was that. Our extended family broke off into their own little pods to begin new traditions, adding new people through marriage and birth and maybe even (gasp) some new recipes. The end of an era. We had held on as long as we could. Such is the bitter and sweet of this physical life. People transition in and out of those chairs around the table whether we like it or not. Some move to new cities; some move on through divorce; and, of course, some move on to that big Thanksgiving table in the sky. We mourn the moving on; we mourn the change; and in that mournful mind-set we just plain mourn the impermanence of living. Those pesky sands through the hourglass. You cannot count on anything to stay the same. Damn it.

But even the end of an era doesn't need to mean it's over. In my family, the people part was easily fixed because of the strong branches of love on our family tree. I threw out some ideas about an annual summer reunion in the Midwest that we now call "Thanksgiving in July." We gather at my cousin Debbi's lake house in Wisconsin. We share a summer feast, catch up on all the latest news, and watch a drop-dead gorgeous sunset from the dock. It's our new ritual, and it fills the void quite nicely as our family love story continues, playing out in front of a new backdrop.

But what was I to do about a plan for the actual day of Thanksgiving? It has become clear that the things I used to be able to count on growing up won't be the same at all, not even close. The guest list will change depending on who is flying into town or who is free that day. I don't eat meat anymore, so there won't be a big bird in the oven, cooked or otherwise. Two years ago, my table was filled with great friends and we drank Bloody Marys and swam in the pool most of the day, ate our meal, and then danced in my foyer until 2:00 in the morning. Last year, my family flew out from Chicago and we did something more traditional. This year we met in Napa Valley. And maybe next year will be entirely different.

So how do I bring that sense of ritual that I love so much to a new day? How do I make the Thanksgiving holiday that I have always cherished my own? How do I capture the spirit of the traditions that wove our family together, even while their form changes? These days, the people I consider family are not all connected by shared DNA, but they mean as much to me.

I gave this a great deal of thought as a new November was nearing. I wanted to create something that would be impervious to external conditions, not dependent upon anything or anyone but me. I didn't want the tension of having to "make something happen" that would be fitting for my favorite holiday based on a past that was decidedly over. If Thanksgiving was not reframed, I could conceivably set myself up for a disappointment. I wanted a sense of rootedness, timelessness, and most especially meaning.

And finally, it dawned on me. I wanted to create the energy of Thanksgiving—and why not have it for the entire thirty days of November so it all didn't hinge on one twenty-four-hour period? The ideas came fast and furious and have since shaped themselves into a spiritual practice. On November 1,

I set out to make appreciation my front-and-center focus for each of the next thirty days. Every sight, smell, taste, conversation, experience, and, most important, person would present itself to me as a gift to unwrap, a treasure to unearth.

Every single morning, for that entire month, I set my intention to see my world and everything in it anew. It took focus to stay present, but I helped myself out by repeating "thank you" like a mantra throughout the day, every day. And soon, my mood lifted, my heart lightened, and awe and wonder were my emotional countenance. I *lived* thank you. A complete and total commitment to embody *thank you*.

For thousands of years, sages from every walk of life have told us that there is gold in those appreciation hills. Now I'm mining that gold and building on that wisdom by creating a forever tradition I will celebrate from November 1 through November 30 each year. What's on the menu and who's at the table on the third Thursday of the month is just going to be a lovely surprise. No pressure to duplicate scenes from the past. My family's love story is being well tended to—and now I have a whole new ritual for the special holiday we once shared.

* * *

I learned from Abraham-Hicks, one of my most cherished spiritual teachers, that appreciation is actually one of the highest vibrations that exist on the planet today. For those of us who have spent our lives writing gratitude journals, the distinction between gratitude and appreciation is worth considering. Abraham explains that appreciation is higher on the vibrational scale than gratitude because with gratitude we are sometimes saying thank you that things are better than they used to be—adding a bit of resistance to our energetic offering. For example, gratitude can look something like "I am so grateful this year isn't as bad as all the other ones." "I am so grateful that I didn't break another bone and there's still no sign of a new tumor." "I am so grateful I didn't go bankrupt and was able to at least pay my bills." "I am so grateful that my friend Susie helped me out of that big fat mess I was in."

Appreciation, the reveling in a thing just for the sake of it, is cleaner, more buoyant, and comes with no strings attached. Appreciation is loving the color green in the yard. Appreciation is thinking about the people we care for and feeling the love for their being—just because. It's noticing the wind on your face, the taste of a snowflake, the smell of cinnamon, the calming sensation of a hot bath with lavender oil. The sunrise. The sunset. The all-is-well-ness of this life. Appreciation is the perfect prescription for melancholy about what has gone before and is no more. Appreciation brings presence, softens mourning, and offers a rising up. And in the rising up I see the passageway to the rest of my wonderful life.

And I am very much appreciating that story.

16

The Love List

*Love never dies a natural death. It dies because we don't
know how to replenish its source. It dies of blindness
and errors and betrayals. It dies of illness and wounds;
it dies of weariness, of witherings, of tarnishings.*

—Anaïs Nin

G iving one's first sermon as a layperson is nerve-racking.
Especially when the occasion is as historic as the first
gay wedding ever to be held at the prestigious New York
Public Library, with a Page Six Who's Who list of attendees.
When it slowly dawned on me the night before, in the midst
of the rehearsal dinner, that my prepared remarks were going to fall short, I raced back to my hotel room, ripped up my
planned wedding spiel, and stayed awake the whole night
rewriting every word.

The four hours I had spent eating and drinking with the two families was a glorious buffet of love, and I had feasted heartily. The following day, at the actual ceremony, I would take my place on the podium with two of my dearest friends, and I wanted so badly to meet the moment. I wanted my words to frame the import of this union and what it said about this time in our country, in our culture. A long time coming, the rights of our fellow citizens to marry were at last being recognized state by state.

This wedding weekend had multiple layers for me. Unmarried, unattached, and feeling unclaimed, I was eager to write a new chapter in my own love story. It was still strange to me to be in the middle of my life and in my present circumstances. I'd searched for relationships to aspire to but couldn't find a bountiful smorgasbord of examples. I admit a scanty few unions I observed seemed pretty good. Some seemed . . . hmmm . . . all right. For many, though, the participants oozed boredom; the relationships looked devoid of any hint of sizzle or even tenderness. But this new coupling seemed different. It showed signs of being the kind of passionate spiritual partnership of beloved equals that I might dream of manifesting for myself. And now, in New York City, I was wondering how to attract and inhabit a fully built beautiful love life like the one I was about to make legal.

I had known one of the grooms, Nate Berkus, for more than

a decade. I met him as his star was just beginning to rise as the "cutie-pie" decorator on *The Oprah Winfrey Show*. He was funny, charming, and so, so smart. We weren't super-close, but we were always friendly. Then came the disaster that upended his life.

In 2004, when the Indonesian Ocean tsunami hit, Nate and his partner, Fernando, were vacationing on a beach in Sri Lanka. I'll never forget the wrenching reports that spread at the speed of light through Harpo Studios. Nate was alive, hallelujah, but Fernando was missing and ultimately presumed lost.

Nate's family and friends gathered at his Chicago apartment shortly after his return. He was fragile and haunted. Nothing could be said that made any sense at all, so instead we just locked eyes wordlessly. He had been through something unspeakable and was fighting for his sanity. The trauma and grief were cataclysmic. But slowly, over time, with help and support, Nate retrieved the essential part of himself and began to live again.

I was splitting my weeks between Chicago and Los Angeles when Nate reached out and told me there was someone special he wanted me to meet. We arranged to have dinner at my rented house in the Hollywood Hills. It is a night that is engraved on my memory. The air was California balmy, and there was a feeling of old-soul magic. It was so good to see Nate again. We'd grown closer over the years, had had some real heart-to-heart talks, and had become an important part of each other's support system. And oddly, this Jeremiah Brent, whom I was laying eyes on for the first time in my life, was feeling like someone I had known and loved for a long, long time. I couldn't shake the feeling.

We talked into the early morning about the Universe and our beliefs, the pitfalls of fame, awful parties, the dream-building energy of Los Angeles, and anything else we could think of to keep the night from ending. As the hours passed, it was as if the energy of their love for each other was expanding and encircling me, too. A surreal, heart-opening experience. As I watched them that night, I had this thought: "What I'm seeing is the true power of the right match. One in which you are still individuals but somehow that 'together piece' astronomically elevates you both." Nate seemed deeply contented in a way he had never quite seemed before. His speech was as smart and hilarious as usual, but it was also infused with a compassionate, sweet humility that felt new. They teased about each other's foibles, and we cracked up over it, but the comments were also dear and loving. And it was clear those imperfections had played a role in drawing them to each other. Being with them that night, I saw a powerful example of how being loved and loving back could be an incredible, purposeful path to betterment.

The third time the three of us met for dinner, they asked me to marry them, and we all burst into tears. Once I understood what they actually wanted me to do, I nodded an effusive yes. In no time at all I was a card-carrying minister of an online church with full authority to bless a union.

The whole experience of "wedding" that happens every Saturday in church halls and country clubs from sea to shining sea is a ritualistic cornerstone of Americana with which I am intimately familiar. On many a June, July, and August day, I have stood in my pointy-toed satin pumps with sweat dripping down my taffeta-clad body at a perfectly gorgeous wedding ceremony. I've been a bridesmaid at least twenty times, with the pastel gowns and matching shoes to show for it. I've been maid of honor three times, too, so I have, in fact, rhymed my way through hilarious, touching, and tear-jerking toasts. When it comes to being a supporting cast member at a nuptial wingding, I have some game.

However, being the actual minister was new territory. I had never written and delivered what would amount to a sermon. That seemed important. I gave it thought, mulled it over for weeks, put something together that I believed was pretty good, planned my outfits, and headed to New York City.

*   *   *

The rehearsal dinner took place in the private back room of the Greenwich Hotel. Stepping through the door, I was instantly enchanted. Beautiful wooden farm tables, twinkling lights, and jaw-droppingly gorgeous buckets of flowers unleashing their perfume all lent to the mood of beauty, inclusiveness, and warmth. Seventy-five of Nate's and Jeremiah's family members and a few close friends were in attendance. I had no real responsibilities other than to sit back, relax, stay fairly sober so I'd be in good form the next day, and feel the love.

And what a love it was. Of course, most couples who are hours away from their marriage ceremony feel like no one ever has been or will be more in love than they. But these guys had a love story that was truly epic.

Nate had just barely survived an international catastrophe and lost a great love. Jeremiah had once lived out of his car in Hollywood, hoping he could build a life worth living. Both had faced tragedy, death, bullying, discrimination, and had grown up with divorce, Jeremiah with abandonment. And like millions of other LGBT people, they had been through the experience of "coming out," claiming their identity and everything that comes with that. They had spent years wondering if they would ever be legally entitled to the whole thing. Marriage. Family. The everyday lifestyle taken for granted as a certain and promised civil liberty by many of the rest of us.

On the flight out to New York City for the wedding, I had flipped to a page in my magazine and gasped. There were Nate and Jeremiah in a "real-life couples" ad for Banana Republic. I hadn't known they had been chosen for this campaign, created not only to sell clothes but maybe to promote some understanding and some acceptance, too. The clearly romantic photograph had a secret mission layered in, a mission to which any superhero might be assigned, and I liked the comparison. With such public careers and an ardent fan base, these guys could actually change hearts. They'd been led, step-by-step, to this great love of theirs. I had the sense that there were more beings involved in this story than the eye could behold. Family and friends from countless generations, Nate's lost love Fernando, angels and bearers of light who had all collaborated to bring these two together at the perfect moment, in the perfect way, so that they could use their superpowers for good.

From across the table, I could see their life together taking shape before my eyes. They were absolutely ecstatic. Their joy cups were overflowing. I remember thinking that if they could capture what they felt for each other right then, in a private detailed narrative, it would be a powerful tool for future use when things got shaky or challenging—one that such notable designers as they might keep in an old antique chest. A way to make time stand still. A reminder. A relic. A Love List.

I realized that for the longest time I'd held a superficial belief that love is like a magical zap that either sticks or doesn't.

But in reality, think about how we all fall in and out of love with each other—lovers, friends, coworkers, even family members sometimes get the boot. It occurred to me that all of us need a way to remind ourselves what someone means to us and why.

A formal Love List gathers all of those reasons, from the "bigs" to the "littles." What you see, feel, sense, adore, respect, admire, honor, delight in. What amuses you. What touches you. What makes your spirit soar. What makes you laugh. What lights you up. What fascinates you. What makes your heart beat faster. In a multitasking, disposable world, it makes sense that we all need a tool to help us stay sharply focused on the best of one another.

As the rehearsal dinner came to a close, plates were cleared and the toasts began. Each family member took a turn at the mic. Something was revealing itself to me. The parade of speakers held my rapt attention as they cleared their throats and wiped their eyes and attempted to get through what they most wanted to say.

These families weren't a gaggle of liberal pioneers who had championed the rights of gay people before being gay began moving toward mainstream acceptance. Nate's family from suburban Minnesota, Jeremiah's from Modesto, California, had pushed themselves beyond cultural norms and had chosen to become enlightened. These were people who, one by one, over time, had adopted a more leading-edge "love is love" view, even when some of America wasn't quite up to speed.

I watched in awe as the hours sped by and person after person rose and paid tribute. Their joy was uncontainable. For each side, each family, their beloved boy had found his true love at a moment in history when finally he could build a life like everyone else. Somewhere along the way, these extraordinary-ordinary moms, dads, brothers, sisters, uncles, aunts, and grandparents had each made a decision that they would support this wholeheartedly. Now, we were gathered in the slipstream of those powerful choices.

When Jeremiah's sweet Santa Claus–like grandpa got to his feet to say his piece, he explained he didn't understand it all, but he did know that he loved his Jer and wanted him happy. And then he wiped his eyes and sat down. It was then that knew I would be up all night rewriting my speech because I had missed the real nugget.

This just wasn't any old wedding. It wasn't just that by falling in love Nate and Jeremiah had elevated each other. The other story was equally riveting. Everyone in their lives had risen up to meet the moment, too. It was a veritable goodness "festival" originating from two good men who had walked through fire to live authentically. Their courage and their commitment to their truth had a transformational impact on everyone around them.

*   *   *

Our lives present us with a never-ending supply of these potentially big shifts. The times when we get a chance to rise in love and be more than we once thought we were capable of being. It's a metamorphosis that asks us to see each human being who stands before us with fresh eyes and hearts. From there we make a habit of donning our magical glasses that focus us toward the good in one another. Then we commit to relentlessly reminding ourselves of that good so we don't risk losing that vision over petty grievances, misunderstandings, or judgmental assessments that seek out imperfection and find it.

Many masters have told us that the most important decision we will ever make is whether or not we choose to see the Universe as benevolent. That decision will shape our lives, as will many others. Faith—that's a decision. And trust. Compassion? Empathy? Hope? Happiness? Some say they're feelings, but more and more I see they're really decisions. Decisions that create outcomes. Love. The biggest decision of all.

On the timeline of humanity, we are in an era where we are being asked to seriously consider the possibility of deciding to love. We can feel it in a quiet moment. All the bad news—the politics, the hate, the division—points to how seminal these times really are. Landmark passages in life like Nate and

Jeremiah's wedding open up a vortex—a momentary respite from all of that ill will—to help make it easier for us to see the path of our own happiness, too. They offer us an opportunity to make a seismic shift, to turn our own magical glasses on ourselves and move closer to our own dreams.

And as for that external rigmarole—what is the answer to all of this unwanted contention on the cable news crawl? The stuff that leaves us worried sick, filled with disdain, and troubled to the depth of our souls? Are we just to wring our hands? Tweet a protest? Meet in the park with a homemade placard and share a hearty battle cry? Maybe.

But I can see with such clarity that, before I don my marching shoes, it would be good to be sure I have risen in love in my own neck of the woods. I can see how crisis, stress, pessimism, fear, anger, and disappointment have often sapped my capacity to love. I can see how not managing those emotions with tenacity can be the start of the slide to a sourpuss way of being that contributes the gloomiest of energies to the whole.

In the midst of an epic love story one night in Manhattan, I faced the truth that, unless I was willing to rise in love in the middle of my life, I would unlikely be the star of my own epic love story.

And I want that role. I want that dream.

*   *   *

When I stepped up to the altar the next day and looked at the love-filled faces of my dear friends Nate and Jeremiah, I told them that I saw this moment not only as a great honor of my life, but a sign that collectively we humans have decided to create a kinder world. And then I spoke to them, and to the assembled guests, about superheroes, the Love List, and magical glasses.

When their vows were said, as I tried to scoot my way out of the camera shot, disaster struck. I accidentally knocked off of the podium the traditional saved-for-the-final-moment-of-the-ceremony Jewish "stomping" glass. The shattering went on forever, accompanied by a collective slow-motion gasp from the three hundred glitterati in front of me.

The grooms and I looked at one another in a moment of panic. Then we doubled over and laughed like crazy.

17

You Gotta Walk Before You Can Pole Dance

You take all sorts of chances in your work,
but you don't take those emotional chances
where your heart is. I want you to do things
where you could be humiliated . . . safely.

—Dr. Laura Berman, sex therapist and love coach, in a session with me

I don't think you want to do it," Nancy says.

I nod emphatically. "I don't think I want to do it."

"I think it's okay," she says, a look of concern and sympathy on her face. "I don't love that idea—for you."

The idea in question is . . . pole dancing. More specifically: *me, pole dancing.* Nancy and I are recording in my favorite room at Belle Vie, the garden room, debriefing about my recent session with love expert, relationship coach, and sex therapist Dr. Laura Berman, during which she suggested I take up the aforementioned activity. Since then, I have been blocking it out. I have missed calls; I haven't returned calls; I've ignored emails. I must really not want to do it.

"I think it's the undulating," I tell Nance. "I think she wants me to undulate."

She shudders visibly. "I don't want you to do that. Can't you use your knee as an excuse? 'My knee hurts. I can't undulate.'"

We both fall out about laughing at the ridiculousness of the two of us trying to come up with excuses for me not to cozy up to a stripper pole as if it were fifth-grade gym class. It's at a moment like this that I literally forget that hundreds of thousands of people are gonna listen to our conversation, since we are recording it for our podcast, *The Sheri + Nancy Show*.

Something has changed in me. I am not nearly as guarded as I've been for much of my life. In fact, I'm trotting out my secret wares, my most heartfelt longings, in a way I used to avoid at all costs. It's also cathartic bringing my crap out from under the bed into the bright light of day, and I am feeling freer. The podcast recording sessions take place in the comfort of my home. Nancy and I sit in comfy slipcovered white chairs listening to the birds sing outside the paned doors, chatting openly and losing track of our inhibitions. Neither of us clicks in to the fact that we have revealed anything super-private until a listener writes in and says, "Sher, Nance, you two are so brave!" We gulp and press on.

It's hard to be cloaked in shame when you are ripping off your own metaphoric clothes and streaking past an audience. I strip down some more in sharing the details of my sessions with Dr. Laura Berman.

Laura and I have known each other for years because of her many appearances on *The Oprah Winfrey Show*. She's a nationally renowned television expert with a shelf of best-selling books, a provocative TV series called *In the Bedroom* that ran on OWN, and a popular radio show, *Uncovered*, during which listeners call in for her advice about their sex lives. She reminds me of Elle Woods—that hilariously upbeat character in *Legally Blonde*—because of her bubbly blond physicality. But her teen-movie-cheerleader looks deceive. She tells it like it is, is embarrassed by nothing, and makes absolutely no judgments about her patients' sexual proclivities.

For our first "sex therapy" session, I arranged to see her on a trip to my old hometown, Chicago. We met at Soho House, a four-story club with beautiful nooks and crannies where creative types flock to do some work or gather with friends. There are also overnight accommodations, and that's where I booked a suite for our meeting. Creating a bit of a therapy "office," I pushed two chairs across from each other, and there we sat and spoke intently and intimately for ninety minutes.

I consider Dr. Berman a friend, but with her professional hat on, after doing an intake Q&A with me, she delivered a piercing analysis of my predicament—my chronic inability to create a fulfilling adult love life.

"You have intellectual prowess matched with full ability to execute, and it is highly unusual to have both to the degree you do," she said. "You have always channeled these gifts in powerful ways. This is an aspect of you that has always been valued by everyone, including your family. Your ability to take things all the way from inspiration to fruition is truly magical. Your left and right brain work beautifully together to match creativity, intuition, and execution in order to communicate in a way people can feel heart to heart."

I straightened in my chair, knowing I was about to find out why all of this stuff that sounded so fantastic was not necessarily a good thing.

And sure enough, the "But" came next.

"But, because your smarts were so highly valued growing up (and the rest of you was not valued enough), you may have undernurtured other parts of you. You now may avoid exploring areas like love, body, relationships, or vulnerability for fear of 'not being good at it.' You find it hard to hang on to your sense of brilliance in the face of what you perceive as failure in any other area. Your fear of humiliation if you fail and get rejected has helped to keep you from trying. If you're in control, you won't be dependent on anyone; you won't be let down or taken unawares. If you're directing things, you can FMC (fix, manage, and control) everything and you won't be hurt. But softening some, letting go of control, and making room for a man to help, serve, assist, and care for you is a key part of attracting a virile, compassionate man."

Her assessment felt accurate, and she delivered it with such compassion that it was easier to hear than I had imagined it would be. The idea of softening feels good. There is no doubt in my mind that I have worked hard to avoid humiliation, which doesn't seem so crazy to me. But what am I to do about it, now that I am ready to rewrite my love story?

Dr. Berman's prescription for me is both easy and awkward. She has asked me to come up with five specific words that describe how I want to feel when I am with said "virile, compassionate man."

That's easy.

My words are *secure, passionate, affectionate, seen, held.*

Then, over the coming weeks and months, I am to connect with those words and conjure up some energy around them. I know I won't find this difficult; I trust it because I know *everything* is energy. Adding the practice of grounding myself in emotive relationship words is a step I am eager to take.

The more gut-twisty, uncomfortable recommendations involve physical practices. Dr. Berman has added private dancing to my homework. I am to dance wildly in my bedroom in front of a mirror, stark naked, and get comfortable with the sensuality of it. And furthermore, she would like me to sample some pole-dancing classes.

I appreciate her reasoning. She's trying to help me recover more of my feminine side and bring some sensuality back into my life in a very practical way. And, as an interesting aside, I know about the value of pole-dancing classes from my time on *Oprah*. Sheila Kelley, a successful actress from such hit series as *L.A. Law* and *Sisters*, actually created a whole system around it. Sheila, who is married to my beloved *West Wing* hero Richard Schiff (Toby for all you *WW* fans), has spent years helping women from all walks of life find their inner love goddesses.

Sheila says, "Every woman has an innate erotic essence that must be nourished, honored, and expressed so that she may be truly free in her magical feminine body."

I would like to feel free in my magical feminine body. I've spent a lot of my life "marshaling the troops," which is, according to Dr. Berman, the make-it-happen masculine energy. For me, a return to some of that divine feminine energy would be a relief. I love what Sheila and Dr. Berman are saying. I love the female/male energy dance. Yes, I want to be on the floor dancing (sans pole) instead of watching from the sidelines tapping my toes. I wholeheartedly agree it would be especially effective if only I would let go a little. Give up "leading." But why is that so hard for me?

Dr. Berman and I take a trip back to my past, where I draw some eyebrow-raising conclusions about myself and my love choices.

Have I ever been with a man who, shall we say, veered toward "appropriate"? Maybe a couple times, but mostly no.

My romantic history has progressed through several distinct phases.

The phase during which I wanted to heal some wounded, implacable, unknowable athletic gods. Unsuccessfully.

The phase during which the words "My wife doesn't understand me" were like catnip. Great for everything but real emotional intimacy. Not to mention far afield of my respect for the virtual Sisterhood.

The phase during which conquering the rascals that droves of other women longed for would perhaps demonstrate my beauty and worthiness—otherwise known as competing for *the player.*

The detective phase during which figuring out the puzzle of him(s) was all consuming. Never daring to ask for clarity or truth. Afraid of the answer.

The phase called "I hope nobody finds out about this," which is why we stay inside and away from daylight.

All that crazy business.

Even during my teenage years, the nice guys who I now see were the real catches didn't capture my fancy. Without struggle and overwrought drama and heart-hurting confusion— *Does he love me? Or doesn't he?*—I was bored. Read: foolish.

But now, with a reckoning under my belt and a love song in my soul, I want to connect with a wonderful man who is just easy to be with. Dr. Berman asked me to describe him in a phrase or two, and I came up with "human cashmere." Cozy, warm, feeling good to the touch. I also want to discover the absolute right love life for me. Full-time? A duo-city travel-back-and-forth kind of thing? Legal marriage? A committed-through-thick-and-thin partnership as long as it works for us both? I don't have that answer, but I am open to what feels best.

Weeks later, in a friendly visit to my home in L.A., Dr. Berman brings a big box of hostess gifts. For years she has had her own booming sex toy business, so I should have been prepared. Soon I'm unpacking a goodly supply of vibrators, crystal "wands," crystal "eggs," goops, and potions.

"Wow . . . Gee . . . Thanks."

Dr. Berman howls, but she's made her point. I need to percolate some sexual energy. (I spend the next week securing an ironclad hiding place so my cleaning lady doesn't stumble onto this mini–sex shop that's ended up in my house.)

Many have tried to coax me into signing up for online dating, insisting it's the only way to meet someone for romantic partnership these days. This is usually followed by a story of how a friend of a friend of a friend met their now-husband online. However, my observation of many women I know who have racked up dozens upon dozens of dates using this strategy tells me cyber-matchmaking is not for me. Too wearying. Kind of depressing. Rarely leading to the connection that ignites a relationship. I've heard lots of cautionary tales, and a few months of that could shut me down for good. Not to mention, I never enjoyed blind dates to begin with, so an endless slew of them isn't an appealing prospect.

Instead, I'm going to let my new love story unfold as it does. And I will continue to ready myself for its arrival. I'll keep opening my heart, dismantling my old armor, and envisioning how it will feel. I've always believed that romance is the delicious frosting on a really great cake. The cake being a well-loved, expansive life. My life today.

For now, I've put the "undulating wildly" prescription on hold, but its value is not lost on me. I think "Excavate your buried feminine sexual self and raise her up" is a message I need very much.

But you gotta learn to walk before you can pole dance.

18

Freedom, Growth, and Joy

In the midst of movement and chaos,
keep stillness inside of you.

—Deepak Chopra

There are few things I would rather talk about than meditation. I like to compare the types of meditation and laundry-list the many proven benefits to anyone who might listen. I might slip into my saleswoman persona and work to convince you of why you should immediately commit to a practice of stillness, even as my buzzing brain searches itself for more ways to make you see its value. Can you see by looking in my earnest eyes how much I believe in it? My meditation of choice is TM (Transcendental Meditation) and I will tell you that it's the easiest thing in the world to do.

What I might not share is that the most challenging part

for me about meditating is not quieting my mind; it's quieting my mouth, sitting still, and meditating.

My family didn't use the word *spirituality* when I was growing up. It's a term that would have been lumped in with something akin to the "dark arts." Our ceremonies were called church. They happened every Sunday and were part of a bigger picture called religion. My mom was raised Methodist, and my dad's family was Catholic; when they married and had me, the Catholic side won.

I have to admit that as a mini-acolyte, I lost interest in the whole shebang pretty quickly. Attending mass on Sunday was one of those "have-tos" forced on me by parents who sometimes, I suspected, felt like they had to, too. At first, there was a novelty to wearing a doily secured by bobby pins on my head, a frilly dress, and shiny patent leather shoes. But after that initial delight wore thin, I struggled to stay awake in a hard-backed pew. I would hope to high heaven that the priest would choose the shorter group prayers so we could get through mass quickly and be on our way home for pancakes.

Once I hit junior high and learned how to play the acoustic guitar, things got a little more interesting. I joined the St. Dismas guitar group, populated by older kids I idolized. They were stylish and sophisticated and rebellious and ridiculously talented. The group sang at the folk guitar mass on Sundays, and I was happy just to be standing beside them in my bell bottoms with my long, straight, middle-parted hair. To be a part of such grooviness.

I mean, looking back, I have no idea why those cranky pastors who ran things didn't show us the door. Our material was pretty edgy. We were belting out "Aquarius/Let the Sun Shine In" by the Fifth Dimension and a load of John Denver. "Let me lay down beside you, let me always be with you" seems like pretty freaky stuff for a seventh grader to perform right next to the altar. But it was the early seventies and looking back now lots of things were a little strange. The lapels on my dad's dark green leisure suit were the size of boat paddles, matched by his pork chop sideburns. Mom, who had a perfectly nice full head of hair, wore a short, frosted wig that pulled on her forehead skin and gave her a headache.

In college, at the University of Iowa, I broke free of the "have-tos." While my new Irish Catholic friend Eileen Callaghan hit the Student Center for mass each weekend and entreated me to join her, I abstained. Catholicism was part of my heritage, the same as being of Polish, Lithuanian, Swedish, Scots-Irish, Canadian descent. But it wasn't my practice. I had already determined that organized religion run by elderly white men wasn't my path, no matter how many times I had been anointed in holy oil.

I spent years perusing the self-help aisles of bookstores, looking for truth. What was the meaning of things? Why are we here? What is the purpose of our lives? I spent much of my tiny monthly budget on a personal library of these self-help manuals as I doggedly tried to find the program or philosophy that would speak to me. Sometimes I would feel a little igniting happening in my soul, and then the fire would fade and I'd resume the hunt.

Then came the moment that put an end to my wandering.

In 1992, Marianne Williamson's first book, *A Return to Love*, was introduced to the world by Oprah Winfrey on her top-rated daytime talk show and was quickly catapulted to phenom status. I wasn't working at the show back then; I was still producing TV commercials, but I'd seen the press about the book and scurried to my local Barbara's Bookstore on the north side of the city to grab my copy. For me as well as millions of others, the message of the book resonated. Marianne was the first to put into clear and accessible language the idea that love was the force above all. It was both the call to action and the endgame. Miracles were shifts in perception. She had brought the concepts of the psycho-spiritual path called A Course in Miracles to the masses.

I mark that as the start of my real spiritual training. Finally, I had the beginnings of a new language and a set of ideas that resonated with me. Wayne Dyer and Louise Hay had warmed me up, but it was Marianne Williamson who raised me up.

Three years later, I was in spiritual grad school with Oprah

it or leave it, which I think is a good sign every time I learn more about the psychology of the modern-day cult.

The language of Abraham is about the connection with your inner being or Source, and that was language that spoke to my soul. The steps are so simple. "Ask. It is given. Allow." The path is shared in a clear-cut manner. "You create your own reality." The identification of our basic needs and desires contained in three perfect words. "Freedom. Growth. Joy." The state of the union? "Everything is always working out for us." The secret to happiness? "Alignment trumps everything." How do you get there? "Meditation is one easy way."

Even all these years later I have not found a better road. The material continues to come in the clearest language I have ever experienced. It's about quantum physics, universal law, and the energy that creates worlds. For me it's the capital Q kind of Quantum, actual Infinite Consciousness, not just theory. I also understand that while I've found my way, one that I share with hundreds of thousands of people around the world, it's not the right way for everyone. Finding the practices and path that set your spirit on fire with joy is a solo job. Sharing it with sister and brother seekers can be fun, but it's not the purpose. It is quintessentially inner work. Between you and *you*.

That is the real beauty of the multicolored woven tapestry of spirit I've come to understand—something I intrinsically felt as a young girl. There is a reason why there are so many languages and paths to Source, God, the Universe, or whatever may be your holy name of choice. Because we are all moving toward the light—physically, psychologically, spiritually—at our own pace, in our own way.

I think there is a litmus test of whether or not a particular path is good for you. A way to dip your toe in the pool before you take the plunge. Ask yourself these questions: Is it loving? To oneself and others? Can you feel yourself rising in energy when you interact with the ideas? Does it allow you and the rest of your human family the ultimate freedom to challenge and question? Does it give you practical guidance to a better life experience? Do you feel free? Do you feel like you are growing in love? Do you feel joy?

Freedom. Growth. Joy. These are the tenets of my path and I think the hallmarks of any authentic spiritual path.

My practice today continues to unfold. Meditation is the foundation. It's the great soother. It takes me out of intellectualizing everything with endless hamster-wheel thoughts that send me straight to made-up stories that accelerate anxiety and worry. It brings me peace, calm, and a sense of reverence about my life. My particular brand of meditation is TM (Transcendental Meditation) as taught by my good friend Bob Roth of the David Lynch Foundation and thousands of other teachers around the world. It is mantra-based and done for twenty minutes twice a day. It has been scientifically tested and found to be extremely powerful in reducing stress when practiced regularly. When I am consistent, everything about my life gets better. Always. But if I allow the noise of the world to move me off center and I begin to think that I just don't have time to quiet my mind, then I suffer. And back to my twenty minutes I go. The remedy is always within reach.

I listen to my Abraham CDs almost every day as my way to stay connected to that universal force that brings me into alignment, and I carve out time for serious daydreaming as a part of my day-in-and-day-out schedule. The art of dreaming has been marginalized, sentimentalized, and devalued when it is really one of the most powerful creative tools we have. A truth I prove to myself over and over again.

When I got serious about my soul, teachers alive and dead, physical and nonphysical began showing up to provide me with ongoing illumination. Thanks to that guidance, I keep discovering new layers of the sacred, the mystical, the ultimate connection. French philosopher Pierre Teilhard de Chardin wrote, "We are not human beings having a spiritual experience. We are spiritual beings having a human experience."

Drop the mic, Pierre.

19

Your Last Three Days on Earth

Though nothing can bring back the hour
Of splendour in the grass, of glory in the flower;
We will grieve not, rather find
Strength in what remains behind

—William Wordsworth (found in my mom's handwriting after her death)

My mother and I lived many lives together. We were each other's darlings until I could speak in sentences. Mortal enemies for a good part of that middle section of preteens through my twenties. In the last long phase, beloveds. Things had softened between us once I found my way into the world of *Oprah*. It was two-pronged—Mom had a much better story to tell her friends (something she cared about), and as a mom, her worry about her oldest child was alleviated. I was on a good solid path in her eyes and pretty much everybody else's.

She and I were complicated for ten thousand reasons, and I can only tell my side of that story now. I'm certain she's fine with that.

One of the things I've noticed about getting older is that the past imprints itself on more and more of the present. Certain seasons, favorite holidays, particular places can never again be experienced without the overlay of loss. As the month of July comes into view each year, I begin to brace myself. The twenty-second is the anniversary of her death, and so many feelings will start to bubble up to the surface. It is still very strange to be parted from her physically, and there are moments when her absence leaves me struggling to breathe. No one on earth cared as much about the intricate details of my life as my mom, Pudge, and I daresay no one else ever will.

Mom lived for five years with Stage 4 lung cancer, even though she'd quit smoking more than twenty-five years before. "So unfair," I think. She had all the treatments: surgery, radiation, chemo (more times than I can count) as she battled for every moment of life she could, holding out for the promise of making it to another vacation, her favorite thing of all. She would want me to say that Pudge was the nickname she was given as a baby because of her infant chubbiness, and that her given name was Marilynn with two *n*s. Everybody in her world called her Pudge except her parish priest, Father Rich, whom she adored. I would tease her and call the good Father

her secret boyfriend, and we would laugh hysterically. "Stop it, Sheri!" she would giggle.

Father Rich was there as her most esteemed guest to give the blessing on the snowy evening of her seventy-fifth birthday. I threw her the most fabulous, fancy party at Spiaggia, a well-known restaurant on Michigan Avenue in Chicago. It was the formal wedding she never had—gilded invitations, men in black tie, women in gowns, a band, a DJ, and a brilliant vocalist to play all of our favorites. I dreamed up the party with our über-talented Emmy-winning *Oprah* production designer, Tara Denise, and we really went to town. Twenty giant white trees on big round dining tables cast a wintry glow around the ballroom. Pudge was center stage. Toasts, poems, and songs were all crafted and delivered in her honor, and like the trees, she was lit from within by the knowledge that so many loved her so much.

When the band struck up my mom and dad's song, "Smoke Gets in Your Eyes," they took to the floor in front of the 120 people who had been among the most important in their lives. It was only when I looked at the photographs later that I saw it: my mom was actually holding Dad up as he quietly wept through the dance. I had thrown the party because I knew in my heart of hearts it would be her last birthday, and I could see Dad knew it, too.

I am beyond grateful that I had the money in my savings

account to follow my impulse and make it happen. I didn't just say "someday" or "maybe I should . . ." and then wonder why I didn't do it in time, like so many other nice ideas that have sailed right by me. It turned out to be one of Mom's happiest days ever, and it will remain for the rest of my life one of the best things I have ever done for anyone. (If you are ever undecided, throw the party. You will never be sorry.)

*　　*　　*

I have run through my mom's final days in my mind thousands of times since. With every year that passes, every July that sneaks up on me with its achingly poignant memories, the lessons of her life and death go a little deeper.

I remember when her mother, my grandma Annie, died, I had an image in my head of my mom being next in line. From my observation, it's a vulnerable kind of feeling when the generation right before you heads off to what awaits us next. Now, being on the front lines myself, I am living with the internal shift where you know you're the next to go. The shift that launches many a midlife crisis or, in my case, a middle-of-life renovation.

That July, she had asked me to drive up from the city and stay the weekend in Lake Villa, Illinois, where she and my dad had made their home for thirty years. Her voice was shaky—a signal to me that things had become dire. The previous week, her doctor had brought up the *h* word—*hospice*—which I knew was the kiss of death. She loved her oncologist, Dr. Hensing, and he had been pulling rabbits out of his hat to keep her alive for five years now. But with no more chemo or therapies to try, she would lose the last shreds of hope she was clinging to and begin to surrender.

We sat on the green plaid couch in the great room while my father, who couldn't overhear us, was in eyeshot.

"You, I worry about less, since you have your spirituality," she whispered. I smiled at the characterization. "But Dad . . . I don't know how he is going to do by himself."

I had observed, over the past year, how she was slowly preparing him for her impending absence. Little Post-it notes appeared on the washing machine and dryer with instructions. Slowly and without fanfare, she would teach him some aspect of domesticity that she knew he was lacking. Months before, I had choked back tears and turned away as he tackled a how-to-iron-your-own-shirts lesson. It struck me as so absolutely poignant that after a fifty-five-year marriage it comes down to the simple stuff.

Mom and I sat together, holding hands, for much of Saturday and Sunday. I could feel her fear. She was afraid of dying, of death. Despite her staunch Catholic faith, at this eleventh hour she was shaky about the idea of eternal life. I wanted to channel the right words to ease her mind just a bit. The last thing she needed was for me to be in a heap—or to have to hold herself together to comfort me. So I dug deep and heard myself talking in a calm, assured, confident tone. The words came easily as I described the transition from the physical to the nonphysical as being as simple as heading to a family reunion. I painted a vivid picture of the big nonphysical gala we would all be attending. Each one of us would arrive at a different time, I explained, but all of us were heading that way to the reunion of all reunions. I reminded her of everyone who was already there, waiting for her—her mom and dad; my brother, John; friends she dearly missed. I assured her that the rest of us were right behind her. We are all coming . . . every single one of us. As we talked that through, I could feel her relaxing, letting go of some of the angst and tension and fear. We even chuckled about the fun we'd have when we were all back together again.

When the proverbial sands are flowing through the hourglass at breakneck speed, the irony is that simultaneously time seems to slow down to that present moment. So in that presence, to spend the time we have left bemoaning how fast it's coming to a close feels profoundly foolish.

"Let's stay in this day, Mom," I said. "We've got this day. You and me and Dad. Who knows who is waking up tomorrow? I'm right here with you, and we have this day. Let's stay right here. Let's not worry about what's happening next week or the week after."

We had lived that brutal lesson with John's sudden death four years before. You get the day you wake up in—maybe, just maybe, that whole day—and that's it. So she and I "stayed in the day" and talked some more.

As the sun set, from her regular perch on the far end of the couch near the kitchen, she instructed me on how to make my grandma's stuffed green peppers for dinner. I stood in the kitchen, faithfully following her prompts. She wanted me to freeze some for my dad, for later.

For after.

At 9:00 p.m., I went to their bedroom to kiss her good night and hesitated at the door, which was ajar. I could see my parents on the bed. Dad lay on his back looking at the ceiling, humming a little sweet tune. Mom, in her nightgown, lay on her side next to him. Her eyes were closed and her hand was on his chest, and he was holding it, patting it. I was transfixed. It will remain in my mind a freeze-frame of perfect love.

That was a good Sunday.

On Monday morning, the nurses from hospice arrived and began to set up their wares. Mom would begin getting some morphine, as she was finding it more and more difficult to breathe. I went home that night and canceled a work trip to Los Angeles I had scheduled for the next morning. My sister-in-law had called, with worry in her voice, and strongly encouraged me to stay in town. The moment she said the words, I knew she was right. Even though the nurses told me there was no reason to believe her death was imminent, there was an energy surrounding us that held an increasing sense of urgency. I poured myself a glass of wine and sat in a cozy little room in my Chicago apartment that I called the library. I could still see the lake from my window on a beautiful summer night.

I thought about the weekend and all the territory we had covered on that green plaid couch. No matter how hard we tried, we couldn't stop wondering how much time she had left. Okay, not six months, but could it be one month? I had felt her next to me trying to figure out in her mind if she could eke out enough days to make the annual trip to Michigan two weeks later for one more sunset on the lake. One more delicious Manhattan on the rocks from a perfectly positioned deck chair. One more pontoon ride, serenaded by the call of her favorite loons. One more evening of Salata family performances and sing-alongs.

"Make sure the oxygen company knows where to send the portable tanks," she requested. Of course I did, though I felt pretty sure we wouldn't be going anywhere. Even if she was still alive, getting her to Land O' Lakes, Wisconsin, was inconceivable. It was over six hours by car. But in that moment there was no other answer: "Yes, Mom."

We talked about a lot of things on that couch, but we steered clear of the truth that was staring us in the face. My mom didn't want to go. Not just a little bit—she really, really didn't want to go. She wanted more time, under any circumstances. No matter what kind of discomfort she had to endure, she wanted to be alive. She wanted more days—not even years, just days.

That wanting was encircling an unspoken but unavoidable truth. Her final lightbulb moment. Her own reckoning. Now, at the end of her days, what would she give to get back all the ones she had wasted. All that unlived life.

Even as her breath was labored, and her strength was leaving her, what she would have given to rewind and reclaim the days that got away from her and do them over. What she would have given to have back the hours she spent worrying about things she couldn't control, worrying about things that ultimately never happened, worrying about what others were thinking about her or about the rest of us. What she would have given to recapture the precious life moments she had lost to the fruitless minding of others' business instead of the tending to her own happiness. I know what she would have given. Anything.

We are all of us heading toward that same seat on the couch. How are we setting ourselves up for our departure? Can we bring to the days we have left an exquisite mad, mad love before we run out of them? That's what I want to know for myself. My middle-of-life quest has given me the insight at just exactly how I've misspent a multitude of mine. On far too many occasions, I surrendered a portion of my allotted time to the false notion that I had one whit of control over others' lives, others' happiness. Letting people, situations, and circumstances just happen to me rather than deliberately choosing them. Treating so many days like "Who cares? There's plenty more where those came from."

But if I awaken tomorrow, I get another chance to course correct. To cherish each breath as I stay in my own happy lane. To release what does not belong to me with loving-kindness. To place my hands on my heart and murmur my thank-yous over and over again. With each new sunrise, another shot at my Mighty DreamQuest.

What will I do with what I know now, with what I saw from the river's edge? What will I do with my mother's last and greatest teaching?

On Tuesday morning, when I drove up from the city, I found her lifeless in bed. We had spent her last three days on earth together.

She would want me to tell you this story.

20

You Are What You Dream

What a wonderful life I've had.
I only wish I'd realized it sooner.

—Colette, French novelist and journalist, 1873–1954

The story is always ours to write. That is the crystal clear, relentless truth. Whether we're aware of it or not, whether we acknowledge it or not, we are writing our story every single day of our lives. I certainly wrote mine.

Some years, my story was about the privilege of serving a worldwide audience, producing television that I felt mattered, feeling so appreciative that I got to spend my days steeped in dream-making.

Other years, I penned a yarn about sleep-deprivation, anxiety, and mountains of pizza, about wondering if opening another bottle of Chardonnay while alone would be a sign of trouble. (It is.) I got to live that fully, too.

As my spiritual life deepened, I could begin to make out the invisible patterns, the mystical tapestry of it all. How a thought would gather other thoughts like it, creating momentum and an outcome. How a chance meeting could lead to a total twist of fate that transformed everything. Then I'd see that it wasn't chance at all, but more like divine intelligence. A story of creation that is being orchestrated by the mix of my well-tended energy field and the limitless field of quantum dreams.

The trick to the full-on joyride is staying in that Big Field. Staying in that wide-open space of light and appreciation and miraculous wonder where most everything you ever wanted surrounds you and the rest is becoming manifested. Keeping your capacity to dream sharp and energized because it is your most powerful creative tool. Not trapping yourself in another blah-blah ho-hum story you can't seem to stop repeating—a choice that will prove, if not fatal, then final.

*   *   *

For a quiet weekend, I have rented a beautiful cottage in my favorite valley on earth to finish these stories. Even in this moment, I wonder what to make of what I've sifted and sorted through in launching, crafting, and living my middle-of-life reinvention, my Mighty DreamQuest.

I've lost dozens of pounds and am driving my aforementioned medical bus toward optimum health and delicious wellness. While I'm not swinging around a pole, I've opened the energetic path and possibility to welcome the man of my dreams for partnership and passionate romantic love. I have shed so many unhelpful patterns of an old life that do not serve my new one.

When I began walking this road, I still believed that transformation was about the destination, reaching the goal, getting to the finish line. Now that I have been living it, I see it is a mind-set, a self-created atmosphere. It's never over. It's entirely about the step-by-step, the moment-by-moment, the next right thing. What's fascinating is that my dreams continue to grow, transform, take shape, become more complex. It's the way our lives are supposed to unfold, delighting us and uplifting us and surprising us. It's not a scientific formula to decipher, but rather a work of art enfolded in mysticism, holiness, and wonder. True-life magic.

I am living my one life dream. For the first time, I am an entrepreneur, a cofounder of a company that continues to take shape, navigating each area of my life by my happiness compass, scheduling myself and my days as I wish. Remembering how free I am now and have always been.

I am feeling eagerly expectant to see where all of this newness goes next, as I prepare to leave my beloved Belle Vie, the home that supported me like a second mother. The beautiful, creeping-fig-covered house where I hunkered down and figured out what I really want and how I might begin to walk in that direction. I am getting ready to say goodbye to the City of Angels—the city where I taught myself how to dream again. I'm leaving because I did what I came here to do and now happiness feels like having a place to plant deep roots. I'm drawn to a lovely small town with a big worldview that I've had my eye on for years.

I scraped the mud from my wings. I cried buckets for the pain I swept into the corners of my life and for the people I have loved so dearly and lost. I felt it all fully. And through that fire, I trained myself to become the worthiest of stewards of my own well-being.

I forgave myself. I forgave others.

I healed. I transformed. I transcended.

How do I summarize the breadth of a full-on reckoning and a redreaming of every area of my life? My leaps forward. My stumbles. My steady progress. I want what I have to say to be as clear as anything I have ever expressed. I keep typing and deleting, typing and deleting. Noodling and noodling some more. I'm at a loss.

On the west side of my weekend retreat, a wall of glass doors opens wide to the outside, and I can see the many creatures who are sharing the space with me. Through the weekend I have taken regular breaks from my writing to be entertained by a mama deer and her babies who play in the field nearby. The trees are awash in chipmunks and squirrels who scamper madly and crush the crunchy leaves with their silly antics. The birds are putting on an air show in perfect syncopation and the whoosh of them swooping and soaring overhead is as regular as an afternoon chime from an old grandfather clock. With the doors open, I feel a bigger wind blowing into the room, and on the tail of that breeze is a dragonfly. She flies about wildly as I look on, startled. Before I can usher her out through the wide open doors, before she can size up the situation and get her bearings, she looks up, sees the sky through the two skylights, and climbs fifteen feet to make her emergency exit. But it's a window, and, of course, there is no way out.

"Oh no," I think. "Don't fly up there! It's an illusion."

For the next several hours, I watch how she psychologically traps herself. It *looks* like blue sky and wide-open space, but every time she tries to reach for it she hits the glass and falls back. Time and time again, she beats her wings until I fear she will kill herself in this fruitless effort. She tries. She rests. She tries the same thing again. Less than ten feet away is her freedom. Everything she wants. Fresh air. Trees. Beauty. The rest of her life. But she can't see it. She won't turn her little dragonfly head over in the direction of what she most wants in the world. She's going to go through that glass come hell or high water. Her one-track mind is holding her prisoner, she won't allow for another possibility, another path. She rests again. I try to free her with a long pool skimmer but worry I might make things worse and damage her gossamer wings permanently, so I stop.

As uncomfortable as her plight makes me, I let her be. For the rest of the afternoon we suffer together. Her trying and resting and trying again. Me trying to close my ears to the heartbreaking sound of her tiny buzzing wings flapping furiously. Finally, I can't stand it and try to make her fly out of the skylight again by waving the pool skimmer. And finally, success! She flies wildly away from the skylight, but then makes another disastrous decision and ends up falling behind the tall steel refrigerator. Now, I worry she has flown to her grave and I will be forced to listen to her last fluttery moments. But a quick swish of a paper towel and her exhausted willingness to let go of her fear and grab onto a lifeline allows her to be lifted out, put under a glass, and walked to her freedom.

She is stunned and exhausted and doesn't move a muscle for a solid three minutes as I stand over her, praying I'm not going to have to conduct a little dragonfly funeral. I hover intently, willing her to make it. Then she moves slightly. She wobbles on her thin little legs, then whirrs her wings and slowly takes to the air like she's had a little too much vodka. I watch her through watery eyes as she rights herself and heads off, more confidently, into the distance. Then suddenly, she flies back to me and circles twice for a final farewell and maybe even a thank-you, which I return. Because I understand what's happened. She's the little helper I've called in to summarize my findings, my learnings, and now my highest knowing.

For many of us, the idea of changing course feels too damn daunting. We are tired; our wings have been beating against a glass pane for a long, long time. We can kind of make out beyond the glass the blue sky we are dreaming of—maybe if we just keep at it, we will eventually break through the barrier. We tell ourselves that it's better just to keep doing the same ol' same ol' than to gather our strength for a new tactic entirely. Even when everything we want is just a few feet away, we can't make ourselves believe it. We can't make ourselves trust it.

Wisdom keepers have been telling us about the wide-open doorway for millennia. They have come in all guises, in all faiths, in all languages. They come one after another to offer their gems to help us break free from the illusion. But lifetime after lifetime, we ignore the simple directions, the map to our own freedom, until *bam*—the big hulking pool cleaner handle knocks us out of our wing-flapping rut and makes us consider a new possibility like making happiness our directional guide, our compass. Or perhaps a beautiful no comes along and breaks our hearts, and we are forced to lay down our resistance, our desperation, and let go.

It is the secret of the secret, the deepest and truest of this life. The formula for a happy life is choosing happiness. Deliberately choosing it. And you know you've done that when you feel good. All the daily, weekly, and monthly practices and choices that create those good feelings are the only tools you need. When you don't feel good, it's time to rewrite the story you're telling yourself. It's time to choose new words, craft a new narrative, stir up some hope. It's time to conjure the tiniest willingness to try something different, to turn ever so slightly in a new direction. And only you can do that for yourself. The simplicity of this truth is its power. Happy people have happy lives. Happy people take better care of themselves. People who take care of themselves deepen their love for themselves. Those happy people who love themselves so completely spill that abundant love all around them into the lives of their dreams.

And we are supposed to live the lives of our dreams.

But there's a choice. Flap your wings against the skylight until you fade away. Or turn your head just a tiny bit to see a new, easier path to the big blue sky. It's just ten feet away. Do you see it? The hand-drawn doorway with the fringy grass and the flower beds on either side?

Now, just walk through.

Appreciation

I have been well loved, championed, supported, taught, bossed, and inspired from my earliest days.

For this book:

What an adventure! My heart is full.

With DreamTribe love to Nancy Hala, who launched a Mighty DreamQuest of her own and a podcast with me.

Grazie mille to the magnificent Ellen Daly for making me so much better, collaborating seamlessly, and coaching me to the finish line.

To Karen Rinaldi, my publisher and editor, your grace and kindness equal your mastery of this art. Your editing is sublime. Your belief has been fuel.

To Jennifer Rudolph Walsh, my stalwart loving friend, you are a legend in a thousand ways. Oh, and then there's your unparalleled literary legacy.

To the stellar HarperWave team—Yelena, Penny, Rebecca, and a shout out to Karen Karbo for helping me mine some early "gems."

For my life:

To my gobsmackingly awesome, world-class singing-dancing family band:

My dear dad, Stan Salata, the master of unconditional love.

My heart sister, Jodi.

My nephews and niece, John, Katie, Grayson, Cole.

Beloved elders: Auntie Barb, Uncle Bob, Auntie Donna, Auntie Margie.

Cousins: Cathy, Brandon, Patrick, Riley, Avery, Caitlin, Christine, Jim, Owen, Wyatt, Ron, Gordana, Allison, Ronnie, Bob, Kim, Claire, Taylor, Joey, Maddie, Julia, Ian, Meg, Paige, Matt, Mark, Jane, Johnny O, Mary Jane, Lily, Amy, Mike, Molly, Jack, Jill, Dave, Danny, Emma, Dan, Hillary, Mitch, Connor, Jan, Greg, Shannon, Damian, Caitlin, Debbi, Bos, Andrew, Brad, Kathleen, Bernie, Jack, Anne, Candie, Lisa, Lori, and all of the new in-laws and greats and great greats.

To my Angel Choir:

Mom, John, Cody, Grandma Julie, Grandma Annie, Grandpa Art, Grandpa Mitty, Uncle Ron, Mary Beth, Shirlee, Jim, and the ancestral realm. Sweet friends, Pam Maier, Ed Morris, Brenda Ziemba, Elissa Strom. You never left.

For years of love and friendship:

To Erin Clark, Perry Stebor, Kathy Schafer, Kathleen Penny, Greg Nicolau, Nate Berkus, Jeremiah Brent, Deneen Brown, Stefanie Kelly, Coral Brown, David Brown, Patricia Miller, Ashley Arnold, Tom Arnold, Courtney Horvath, Alex

Hayano, Olivia Hayano, Thomas Sassane, and sweet Carmen.

To My Soul Sisters—the Alpha Delta Pis of the University of Iowa: Schaf, Simmons, Harman, Callaghan, Arkin, Corsale, Winter, Russell, McCallum, Reiland, Maher, Bennett, Oetting, Bohaty, Finney, the Bernebeis, Esping, Wells, Horsfall, and the rest of the best house evah. Violets.

For the trip to Oz:

With heartfelt thanks to Oprah Winfrey for many, many favorite things.

To the Harpo staff and crew. We gave all. We cared beyond. You were my dreammates through a once-in-a-million-lifetimes experience.

To Harriet for "cleaning" out that old closet. To our "Lincoln-loving" assistant director, Dean, who lived in my ear for five years. To Tyrone, the caretaker. To Tim B., the best man ever. To Sir Tom Stacker, who kept us safe and sound. To Erik for the funnies, et al. To Kim Lorenz and Carla Bird who ferociously assisted and protected. To Mona Antwan for the inspiration. To MoneyP—my work heart for twenty years.

To the dedicated people I served with on the OWN team. You persevered, rose up, and triumphed. Bravo.

For the wisdom, the support, and the inspiration:

To Deepak Chopra, Elizabeth Gilbert, Dani Shapiro, Brene Brown, Arianna Huffington, Kris Carr, Dr. Laura Berman,

Angela Manuel Davis, Jerome Davis, Kris Carr, Colette Baron Reid, Gordana Biernat, Mark Groves, Kylie McBeath, Agapi Stassinopoulos, Lori Harder, Kimberly Snyder, Kute Blackson, Brooke McAlary, Amy Jo Martin, Christy Whitman, Christine Lang, Sonia Choquette, Charles Chen, Marcia Weider, Marci Shimoff, Mel Robbins, Geneen Roth, Martha Beck, Seane Corn, Cheryl Richardson, Kathy Freston, Marie Forleo, Gretchen Rubin, Mastin Kipp, Kala Faulkner, Gary Vaynerchuk, and Happy Money's Ken Honda

To Jana Michael, Dean Sarah Gardial, and Lynette Marshall for bringing me home to Iowa City. Go Hawks!

To innkeeper Matt Barba and team at the world-famous Deerpath Inn for your hilar IG and always giving me a home in Lake Forest, Illinois.

To Ben Weprin and Graduate Hotels for the portrait "honor" and for giving me the perfect locations where I could hunker down and write a book.

To my fellow Jack Benny 39ers.

To the magnificent Carmel High School class of '77.

To Rodger Hedges, Don Dubin, Sister Mary Sattgast, Ms. Betlinski, Mrs. Meng, Mrs. Marshment, Mr. Anacker, Mr. Schmidt, Mr. Myers, and Rabbi Jay Holstein.

To Jack Canfield, Arielle Ford, and the awe-inspiring TLC tribe.

To JJ Virgin, Cynthia Garcia, and The Fabulous Unicorns.

Appreciation

To We Care, Susana, Susan, Renee, Shaman Mari, Yogi Patricia.

To Bridgette O'Connell Becker of Taproot Energetics.

For my Path:

To Esther Hicks, Jerry Hicks, Tracy Ayers, and Abraham—my connection, my light, my forever guides to freedom, growth, and joy.

Notes

Chapter 4: The Mighty DreamQuest

61 loosen their death grip.": Lori Harder, *A Tribe Called Bliss* (New York: Gallery Books, 2018), p. 54.

Chapter 7: OMG! I Forgot I Had Cancer!

102 "staff up posthaste.": Kris Carr, *Crazy Sexy Diet* (Guilford, CT: Skirt, 2011), p. 6.

Chapter 8: I Did Everything Wrong (and It Turned Out All Right)

124 "life within you, all the time.": Joseph Campbell with Bill Moyers, *The Power of Myth* (New York: Anchor, 2011), p. 114.

Chapter 17: You Gotta Walk Before You Can Pole Dance

230 "her magical feminine body.": Sheila Kelley, on her website, https://www.sfactor.com/sheila-kelley/, accessed Jan. 2018.

Dear Reader,

Welcome to . . .

The Beautiful No Experience: A Companion Workbook.
My hope for *The Beautiful No* is to be an offering of
possibility and inspiration to readers around the world. To
share a new vision for the second half of life by telling my
own story about reimaging everything. That in a culture
that telegraphs midlife should be about shutting down, how I
began to dream thrilling new dreams for myself. This in-
depth workbook has been designed to help you do the same.

For years, I had a front-row seat to some of the most
prolific authors, teachers, and wisdom sharers of our time.
What I learned from that experience is that reading about
transformation and watching TV shows about transformation
(not to mention producing them) isn't the same thing as
being transformed. The "being" piece is the crucial part
we sometimes miss. At some point we have to rise up and
become the "experts" of us. Why not now?

Since *The Beautiful No* was first published, I've connected
with thousands of women and men who resonate with the

messages I shared. So many of us are yearning for a better experience of our own lives. And because we live in a world that is transforming in a million ways much more rapidly than we may be used to, so many of us are also grappling with the same doubts, anxieties, and fears.

For my part, I intend to stay curious, optimistic, and hopeful that we are clearing out an old stagnant and unproductive energy to make way for something so much better. Better for all of us.

Whether we acknowledge it consciously or not, we are connected. From every single one of us to our families and friends to our workplaces, towns and cities, to our country and finally our planet. And since evolution is mandatory, we are truly all in this together.

This workbook has been created to support you in taking your next steps on your own profoundly beautiful path of evolution, similar to what I write about in *The Beautiful No*. You'll find questions inspired by each chapter to help you discover where you're at now in your life and where you might want to go next.

Here's to your Beautiful No experience.

Sheri Salata,
February 2021

Tell Me Your Story and I'll Tell You Mine

I have honored the impactful nature of stories for a long time, but it's only now in the middle of my life that I understand their awesome quantum power. I can see clearly now that stories are the actual building blocks of our lives. They are the ingredients of our intentions, our deepest desires, our requests to the Universe, our hopes, our most fervent prayers. And the most crucial stories are the ones we author for an audience of one, ourselves. That's right, what we say to ourselves about ourselves—about every area of our lives—is life and death. The difference between the joy ride and the hard road. (page xviii)

Throughout *The Beautiful No*, Sheri talks about the power of storytelling as she sets out to create a new story for her life.

What is the current story of your life? Write five honest sentences that paint the overall picture. This describes the general state of your life (we'll break it down further in the chapters that follow).

1. _____

_____

_____

_____

2. _____

_____

_____

_____

3. _____

_____

_____

_____

4. _____

_____

_____

_____

5. _____

_____

_____

_____

If Not Now, When?

*Creating a new vision of your life while you are
smack-dab in the middle of it is a bold choice.
Gathering up the courage to step out and think up
new possibilities, having lived through decades
of life, is very different from the wide-eyed
dreams of a kid who hopes someday to become
someone and do some big something. (page 11)*

In the very first chapter, Sheri shares a sobering exercise
many great teachers have used to get students to take stock
of their lives. Sheri found it so powerful, it launched an inten-
sive reckoning of her life, which led to a major epiphany. See
where it leads you.

Find a quiet space and close your eyes.

Visualize a graveyard and walk among the tombstones until you find your own. On the tombstone is one big headline: the lead story of your life.

What does it say?

_____

_____

_____

What do you wish it said?

_____

_____

_____

If you are in the middle of life—let's go deeper. Excavate your beliefs about this time.

What are the messages you've picked up from the culture?

Are you going into the second half of life filled with promise and possibility? Or are you heading toward the finish line of life wearing comfortable shoes and hoping you'll be useful to someone? Are you afraid that the best part of life is over? Zero in on your true feelings here.

_____

_____

_____

_____

_____

_____

_____

_____

_____

_____

Whether or not you are in the middle of life, it's important to see what you've put on hold waiting for "someday."

What's on your someday list?

_____

_____

_____

_____

_____

_____

_____

_____

2

The Reckoning

*The process of reinventing yourself and
revisioning your life requires not only courage but
a deep sense of compassion we don't ordinarily
shine on ourselves. . . . It's the reckoning that
launches the dream. (pages 16–17)*

In this chapter, Sheri shares a process she walked through called "the reckoning." She began by identifying what mattered most to her, and then, with tender eyes, she examined what she had created area by area—body, spirituality, love, career, friends.

Deep breath.

Take a reckoning of your own life. Area by area, begin to assess what you've created so far. Where have you kept your word to yourself? What do you wish was different? What are you proud of? What gives you satisfaction and contentment, and what makes you feel incomplete or unaccomplished?

_____

_____

_____

_____

_____

_____

_____

_____

_____

_____

_____

_____

_____

_____

_____

_____

After her reckoning, Sheri writes about an epiphany that gave her a wake-up call: "The bottom line is this: I have been an untrustworthy steward of my own well-being."

Consider your own stewardship of your well-being. What are the areas of your own life where you've been an unworthy steward? Where do you wish you could do better?

_____

_____

_____

_____

_____

_____

_____

_____

_____

_____

_____

_____

_____

_____

_____

_____

3

My Pink Life

*Letting go. I am starting to see it as the secret
to renewal. And it is also the part requiring
some true grit. An authentic joyride doesn't
allow room for serious baggage. I think it's
a carry-on kind of situation. (page 40)*

Sheri writes about the opening-night shamanic ceremony she experienced at a detox retreat in the Mojave Desert. This exercise provides a way to free yourself from the past and manifest new dreams. To prepare for this ritual, Sheri makes a list of everything holding her back, everything that doesn't serve her, and then, during the ceremony, places it in the fire to Let. It. Go.

You can try this ritual at home. Make a list of the things you want to let go of—things like anxiety, things you're afraid of, people or beliefs that don't support you, negative stories you tell yourself about yourself—all of it. The limiting beliefs that have held you back, the relationships that have drained you. Release your own anger, despondence, hopelessness.

Make a fire in a safe place (your fireplace or barbecue pit will do), and add a little dried sage or lavender to it, if you wish to add a sense of ceremony. You can also just find a safe spot and use a lighter or a book of matches. Then place your list in the fire and watch it burn as you imagine everything on your list dissolving into the air with the smoke. Really let go—imagine yourself releasing all those emotions that don't serve you.

What's on your list of things you are willing to let go of?

_____

_____

_____

_____

_____

_____

_____

_____

4

The Mighty DreamQuest

*Upliftment is a game of back and forth, and it
requires that all parties suit up and play well. Once
you commit to a better-feeling life experience, all the
old negative ways of bonding with others stick out like
crazy. You wonder why you would ever waste your
time making yourself and others feel bad. You see
that commiserating about unwelcome circumstances
is a zero-sum situation. Nobody wins. (page 60)*

Sheri talks about how she teams up with her longtime
friend Nancy Hala to support each other in reimagining
their lives. Sheri refers to this as "intentional friendship."

An intentional friendship is a connection with somebody

who's willing to commit to a relationship of mutual support rather than one of commiseration and gossip. You support each other in creating new dreams instead of rehashing the same old stories you've covered for years.

How can you take responsibility for focusing your conversations on your dreams and goals rather than on gossip and commiseration?

_____

_____

_____

_____

Identify someone in your circle now who would support you in elevating your life. Who do you think would be game? That's your intentional friend.

_____

_____

_____

_____

_____

If you don't have someone in your life right now, here are some suggestions for identifying intentional friends so you can begin to support them and be supported by them.

- Start small! Practice sharing one goal you have, or ask someone what's important to them, just in the course of your daily conversations with the people who cross your path. When the checkout person at Trader Joe's asks you how your day is going, say something that inspires you!
- Invite a friend to meet for a cup of coffee, and try asking them a question about their life that you wish someone would ask you. Be open to having a new conversation!
- Go big! Sign up for a class to develop your skills or express your talents in something you've always dreamed of doing. You'll meet like-minded people and may be drawn to somebody who shares your interests and is super positive and inspiring!

5

Chasing Beauty

The damage went far deeper than fried hair
and a peeling face. Somewhere in this decades-
long "prettiest" toxic mess, I had come up
with a shadow belief that beauty as defined by
others was directly tied to being happy and,
even worse, being lovable. (pages 70–71)

Sheri recalls how even as early as third grade she had an awareness that the tides were shifting—that certain boys and girls were "cute" and that "prettiest" was the most desirable. From there, she developed a whole false story about the power of physical beauty, which launched a series of misguided attempts to obtain it.

How do you define beauty? What kind of things does the voice in your head say to you about your physical appearance: your face, your hair, your body, your clothes, your weight?

_____

_____

_____

_____

_____

_____

_____

_____

Growing up, what did you believe about your physical appearance? What was your childhood beauty story?

_____

_____

_____

_____

_____

_____

What was your young-adult beauty story?

_____

_____

_____

_____

_____

_____

What is the beauty story you wish you could tell yourself right now?

_____

_____

_____

_____

_____

_____

_____

_____

_____

6

Feel the Burn

For those of us in the middle of life, we're in red
zone territory now. This is no longer about wearing
the daring, somewhat-bare dress to whatever
occasion or hitting an important birthday at a
lighter body weight so we don't go off the deep
end. This is now about the very quality of the
rest of our minutes on earth." (page 85)

Regarding fitness, Sheri observes that there are two
kinds of people. The first group she calls "the day-
in-and-day-outers"—people who wouldn't skip their
workout even if that means keeping the happy hour gang
waiting. And then there's the second group—the ones
who share Sheri's fitness story, those who have to drum

up the strength for a "do-over" every four to six months.

What has been your fitness story?

_____

_____

_____

_____

_____

How can you rewrite your fitness story? What five to ten words describe how you'd like to feel in your body right now?

_____

_____

_____

_____

_____

_____

_____

_____

_____

7

OMG! I Forgot I Had Cancer

*I had all of the information I needed to do a thorough
reckoning about my health, but instead of taking
a deep breath and making that commitment to
myself, most of my good intentions went right to my
"someday I'll get this together" list. (pages 96–97)*

Sheri reveals that she had completely forgotten she had
been diagnosed with malignant melanoma and had exten-
sive surgery years ago. It was just one of several wake-up calls
about her physical health.

Have you neglected your well-being? If so, how?

_____

_____

_____

_____

_____

_____

_____

_____

_____

_____

Create a new vision for your healthier life. What are you eating? What kind of movement do you do in a week? How do you navigate stress? How do you bring calm to your life? Who would be on the health-and-wellness team of your dreams? Do you have an ob-gyn, acupuncturist, weight-loss coach, workout instructor, yoga teacher? How can you take advantage of the free wellness advice of top experts (i.e., plant-based chefs, personal trainers, functional medicine doctors) on social media?

What are three easy changes you could make in your daily life that you know would be healthier and contribute to your well-being?

1. _____
   _____
   _____
   _____
   _____
   _____
   _____

2. _____
   _____
   _____
   _____
   _____
   _____
   _____

3. _____
   _____
   _____
   _____
   _____
   _____
   _____

8

I Did Everything Wrong (and It Turned Out All Right)

I believe we all have an inner compass, a directive that lives quietly behind the scenes and really is the mastermind behind most of our life decisions. This compass is a kind of patterned inclination—do we generally lean in the direction of the good stuff, or do we give our compass some attention and rechart our course only when we've made a mess of things? When engaged proactively, our inner compass can help steer us toward good-feeling opportunities that creative positive outcomes. "Where do you want to go?" you say to yourself. "Toward more happiness," you decide. It sounds obvious, but without that deliberate conscious choice, we set ourselves up for a bumpier journey that takes us a long way around to where we really want to go. (pages 111–12)

When you think about your life and your life decisions, can you identify what has been your North Star? What has determined the direction of your life so far, leading you to the choices you've made? (i.e., outrunning anxiety, trying to feel good enough, living up to someone else's dreams for you, wanting to fit in with the crowd, aligning with cultural expectations of what your life should be.)

This is your internal compass.

Looking back on your life, where has your internal compass been pointing?

_____

_____

_____

_____

_____

_____

Sheri writes about how she had unwittingly made misery her compass. Only when she was truly miserable did she know it was time to make a change. Is that something you can relate to?

It may be a big adjustment, or you might be off by just a few degrees, but what would happen if you pointed your compass toward happiness—whatever that means to you? And if you already feel like you lean in the direction of happiness as your North Star, push yourself further and then imagine the impact on your life.

_____

_____

_____

_____

_____

_____

_____

What would you do differently if happiness were your compass? Is there some area in your life where you could make a start today?

_____

_____

_____

_____

_____

_____

_____

9

The Beautiful No

*If we could collapse time and recognize the beauty
in a no right when it arrives, no matter how
disappointed we might feel, I think we would have
mastered something fundamentally important
about living happily ever after. (page 138)*

This one can be a real game changer.

Let yourself think back on your disappointments and heartbreaks. The times you were hoping for a yes and you got a no instead. A disappointing ending to a romance. A divorce. A job interview that didn't go your way. Anything you really, really wanted and felt heartbroken not to receive.

Can you look back now and see how the universe was

nudging you toward a more magnificent outcome? Can you see how the gift of that no propelled you to something that you truly wanted? That is a beautiful no.

Find one beautiful no in your life.

_____

_____

_____

_____

_____

_____

_____

_____

_____

_____

_____

_____

_____

_____

_____

_____

10

The Greatest Show on Earth

*We often don't know we are in the midst of some
truly glorious days until we grow older and more
reflective, and then we gnash our teeth but good. Why
didn't we know how great we had it? Why didn't we
savor those experiences? Why didn't we realize we
were in the best part of our lives? (pages 143–44)*

In this chapter, Sheri recalls her glory days as the executive
producer of *The Oprah Winfrey Show* and especially the glorious production of the very last *Oprah Winfrey Show* ever.

We all have our glory days—what we now, looking back,
might consider peak experiences. They teach us to appreciate
what we had or what we accomplished in the past and also to be
looking forward right now to the glory days to come.

Take a moment to feel appreciation for the glory days in your life.

Choose three instances from your own life that you would consider glorious. Try to remember the details. What did you do? How did you feel? Did you appreciate those experiences at the time?

1. _____
_____
_____
_____
_____

2. _____
_____
_____
_____
_____

3. _____
_____
_____
_____
_____

What are the glorious things bubbling up in your life right now? Write down the details of each one, with an emphasis on appreciation.

_____

_____

_____

_____

_____

_____

_____

_____

_____

_____

_____

_____

_____

_____

_____

_____

_____

_____

My Epic Fail at Work-Life Balance

*In any given moment of our lives, we are deciding
what matters most to us. We direct our attention and
energy to whatever that is. It's a dance of flow, not a
pie chart or a mathematical equation. (page 158)*

Having been asked about work-life balance for years,
Sheri writes about her epiphany that might fly in the
face of cultural norms.

After reading this chapter, what was stirred within you as
relates to the concept of work-life balance?

———————————————————————

———————————————————————

_____

_____

What is the best story you can tell yourself about work and the rest of your life? What is the most empowering language for you?

_____

_____

_____

_____

_____

_____

_____

_____

_____

_____

_____

_____

_____

_____

13

Kissy the Underdog

Even now, as I tweak my recipe for the life of my dreams, there are, of course, days when my middle-of-life reinvention feels like a big mountain I still have yet to summit and moments of frustration when I find it all too much. (page 188)

Through the lens of caring for her English bulldog Kissy, Sheri writes about reinvention, love, and devotion. She ends the chapter with "Kissy's Rules for a Happy Life."

Can you begin to imagine your rules for a happy life? Try to crystallize at least five that could begin your personal recipe.

1. _____
   _____
   _____
   _____
   _____

2. _____
   _____
   _____
   _____
   _____

3. _____
   _____
   _____
   _____

4. _____
   _____
   _____
   _____

5. _____
   _____
   _____
   _____

14

Anatomy of a Rut

*To some extent, big or small, so many of us feel
emotionally dulled and unenthusiastic, and we
aren't sure why. Especially in the middle of life,
aka the been-there-done-that era. (page 193)*

S ometimes we fall into ruts. We don't mean to, but we do.
We accidentally get routinized and find ourselves doing
the same things, the same ways, over and over.

Sheri writes about beginning to stir up "fresh joy" in her
life, in both small ways and big; taking new routes instead of
familiar pathways; and actually tackling things she'd always
wanted to do from her "someday list."

What can you move off your someday list to right now?

Perhaps it's taking a class, learning a new language, or traveling to another country. What about those tango lessons, riding a bike, or running a 5K race? Fresh flowers you buy for yourself every week?

Write down five big things and five small things you can do to mix things up and give yourself a heaping dose of fresh joy.

FIVE BIG THINGS I CAN DO

1. _____

_____

_____

_____

_____

2. _____

_____

_____

_____

_____

3. _____

_____

_____

_____

_____

_____

_____

4. _____

_____

_____

_____

_____

5 _____

_____

_____

_____

_____

_____

_____

FIVE SMALL THINGS I CAN DO

1. _____

_____

_____

_____

_____

_____

2 _____

_____

_____

_____

_____

3. _____

_____

_____

_____

_____

4. _____

_____

_____

_____

_____

5. _____

_____

_____

_____

_____

15

Thanksgiving Redux

*Our lives are bettered by ritual. Ritual makes
things matter as it blesses the ordinary and
elevates it to extraordinary. (page 208)*

Sheri writes about reimagining her annual Thanksgiving
holiday after her move to the West Coast. As circumstances change, she is creating new rituals to provide that sacred layer to holidays—and even to her experience of each
day.

Have you created rituals in your life? What are they?

_____

_____

_____

_____

_____

Begin to imagine new ways to bring ceremony, ritual, and meaning to your daily experience—how you make a cup of tea, choosing the fragrance in your home, making space in your day for mindfulness.

What can you incorporate into your life right away? List new ideas here.

_____

_____

_____

_____

_____

_____

_____

_____

16

The Love List

*In a multitasking, disposable world, it makes
sense that we all need a tool to help us stay sharply
focused on the best of one another. (page 220)*

One way to remind ourselves of what someone means to
us, and why, is to create what Sheri calls a "Love List."
This list gathers all the reasons from the "bigs" to the "littles."
What touches you. What lights you up. What you see, feel,
sense, adore, respect, admire, honor, and delight in.

Choose three people in your life and create a Love List
about them.

Person 1: _____

_____

_____

_____

_____

_____

_____

Person 2: _____

_____

_____

_____

_____

_____

Person 3: _____

_____

_____

_____

_____

_____

17

You Gotta Walk Before You Can Pole Dance

"Every woman has an innate erotic essence that must be nourished, honored, and expressed so that she may be truly free in her magical body."

—Sheila Kelley, actress and thought leader (page 230)

What is your current story about your sensuality?

_____

_____

_____

If you could transcend all of the issues that may be holding you back from fully inhabiting your body and experiencing your "erotic essence," what would your new story be?

_____

_____

_____

_____

_____

_____

_____

_____

_____

_____

_____

_____

_____

_____

_____

_____

_____

_____

18

Freedom, Growth, and Joy

*Meditation is the foundation. It's the great
soother. It takes me out of intellectualizing
everything with endless hamster-wheel thoughts
that send me straight to made-up stories that
accelerate anxiety and worry. (page 242)*

If you have dabbled in meditation or have meditated at some
time in your life, would you consider making that practice
consistent? What are the benefits you have experienced from
meditation?

_____

_____

_____

_____

_____

_____

_____

_____

_____

_____

_____

_____

_____

_____

If you have never meditated, it might be something you want to try as a component to your personal recipe for happiness.

RESOURCES FOR BEGINNING A MEDITATION PRACTICE

GUIDED MEDITATION

Headspace app: headspace.com

Abraham-Hicks:

 abraham-hickslawofattraction.com/meditation
 -3920.html

Transcendental meditation: tm.org

19

Your Last Three Days on Earth

*Can we bring to the days we have left an exquisite
mad, mad love before we run out of them? That's
what I want to know for myself. My middle-of-life
quest has given me the insight at just exactly how
I've misspent a multitude of mine . . . Treating
so many days like "Who cares? There's plenty
more where those came from." (pages 253–54)*

Imagine your last three days on earth and the kinds of
thoughts you might have knowing your time in this life is
running out.

What areas of your life would remain unlived if you don't
make changes now?

_____

_____

_____

_____

_____

_____

_____

Where are the corners of your unlived life that are now your richest opportunities? Knowing passionate love? Adventurous travel? Deep and meaningful friendships? Living an abundantly healthy lifestyle? Expressing your gratitude and appreciation?

Describe whatever comes to mind here.

_____

_____

_____

_____

_____

_____

_____

_____

_____

20

You Are What You Dream

*The story is always ours to write. That is the crystal
clear, relentless truth. Whether we're aware of it or
not, whether we acknowledge it or not, we are writing
our story every single day of our lives. (page 255)*

Put aside your shadow beliefs that have been holding you
in place.

Let go of the suitcases of emotional baggage that you have
been dragging with you on your life path.

What is the most blissful, joyful story you can begin to
write about your life?

About the Author

Sheri Salata is an author, speaker, and producer. Her action-packed days as executive producer of *The Oprah Winfrey Show* were chronicled in the acclaimed docuseries *Season 25: Oprah Behind the Scenes*. Sheri also served as co-president of Harpo Studios and OWN, the Oprah Winfrey Network. Sheri has been named one of Fast Company's 100 Most Creative People in Business, the *Hollywood Reporter*'s Women in Entertainment Power 100, and a 2017 Feminist Press Power Award winner. She is a graduate of the University of Iowa.